Dangerously In Love With His Bestfriend

Cardi' Heart's

Published by Cardi' Heart's, 2024.

While every precaution has been taken in the preparation of this book, the publisher assumes no responsibility for errors or omissions, or for damages resulting from the use of the information contained herein.

DANGEROUSLY IN LOVE WITH HIS BESTFRIEND

First edition. December 13, 2024.

Copyright © 2024 Cardi' Heart's.

ISBN: 979-8230560883

Written by Cardi' Heart's.

~I was a girl who just had things handed down to me. I never had to look over my shoulder or worry about a meal. I met the love of my life, Phil, in college. He wasn't the type I would go for. I was more for the good grades, football or basketball type of boy. But, he was different. His love felt real. The way he treated me was the thing in life I needed. He filled me with so much joy. And when I lost that man of mine. I lost me. I struggled for years to find myself again. Then when I opened my clothing store across another man Killa. He was way different than Phil. We argue most days and he was a cheater. When I found out what he did to my baby. I was scared and didn't know what to do. But, fuck me talking let's get into my story. Starting off 6 years into my life after I lost Phil~ Zara

Chapter 1

6 years later

Zara was nestled comfortably in her living room, the soft glow of the TV casting a warm light around the space as she enjoyed her favorite show. The clock on the wall chimed 9 PM when suddenly, a knock echoed through her cozy apartment, breaking the tranquility of the evening. With a smile spreading across her face, she rose from her seat and approached the door. As she opened it, she was greeted by Killa's familiar presence. "Hey," she exclaimed, stepping forward to wrap her arms around him in a warm embrace, savoring the moment. "Sup baby?" he replied, planting a gentle kiss on her cheek, which sent a flutter of happiness through her. Their chemistry was undeniable; they had been inseparable for the last three months since her shop had opened directly across from his bustling barbershop.

"You're smelling good, as usual," Zara complimented, catching a hint of his cologne as she shut the door and walked back into the living room, Killa following closely behind. His smile was infectious as he responded, "Shit, you stay smelling good," making her chuckle in delight. "Thirsty?" she asked, glancing over her shoulder at him. "Nah, I got my drink right here," he said, reaching into a small bag he had brought and pulling out a sleek bottle of liquor, pouring himself a generous glass.

Zara turned to her refrigerator, opening the door to reveal a selection of beverages. She chose a bottle of her favorite red wine and retrieved a glass from the cabinet, the delicate clinking sound echoing in the quiet room as she moved. As she entered the living room again, Killa was already engrossed in picking out a movie to watch together.

However, her enjoyment quickly turned to dismay as she approached and saw him selecting a scary movie. "Hell no!" she exclaimed, shaking her head animatedly. Killa laughed heartily, his eyes sparkling with playful mischief. "What? Are you scared?" he teased, leaning back in her plush couch.

"I just don't do many scary movies," she confessed, her laughter blending with his. The lighthearted banter filled the air, the comfort of their friendship evident in their easy dialogue. "Yo ass is staying if we're watching this," Killa declared, declaring his intention as he confidently pressed play. Zara couldn't help but roll her eyes but felt a deep sense of affection for the moment they shared, settling in next to him, ready to face the frightful adventure on the screen together as Halloween came on. Zara grabs her blanket getting on the couch next to him. "Come here," he said grabbing her and moving her across his legs so she could lay. "Scary ass," he said

"Shut up," she put the cover over her as he touched her leg with his left hand. Both of their eyes shifted toward the TV as the movie begins.

An hour later

Zara was scared as hell having the cover over her mouth. "Shit'll leave her ass too," Killa laughed, seeing her all scared and shit. He was the type to be scared of movies. He just enjoyed the way they played the shit out. "You dead ass wrong," Zara looked at him, then smiled. "If you see me run. Do what black people do. Run with their ass don't even look. You know how it is"

"No, he just left her. So yo ass would leave me?".

"Damn near," laughing, he leaned over, kissing her on the cheek. Knowing she can be a bug ass baby. Nah I'm just playing. I can't do you like that," he said, looking at her in the eyes.

"Awe okay. Cause we were gone have a problem" He grabs her chin, kissing her. "Shit, I ain't letting no nigga touch you. Well, white man," he says as they both laugh. "I don't know why you holding out on a nigga" he said referring to them having sex. As Killa sat across from Zara, he could sense the weight of her struggles. Their conversation took a serious turn as Zara hesitated to fully engage in their budding relationship. "You know why," she admitted, the vulnerability in her voice reflecting a deep-seated fear rooted in her past. Killa listened intently, understanding that the scars from her previous relationship ran deep, leaving her apprehensive about intimacy. After a three-year absence from that chapter of her life, she still felt the lingering shadows of her history.

Zara had wanted to take her time with Killa, to open up at her own pace. "Yeah, I know it's been three years," Killa replied, trying to reassure her. "Obviously, you ain't with the nigga no more. His loss." But as the words left his lips, Zara's demeanor changed entirely. Her face fell, and the light in her eyes dimmed as painful memories washed over her.

"He died, Killa," she revealed, her voice trembling with emotion. Zara's heart ached as the image of that horrific night flooded her mind, the memory searing into her consciousness. She recalled the chilling sight of Phil, her former partner, lying motionless with blood spilling from a gunshot wound to his head. The vision haunted her for months, and even now, it felt like a shadow creeping into her present. "Damn, I'm sorry," Killa responded, genuine concern etched across his face. "What happened?"

"He was shot in the head," Zara explained, her voice barely above a whisper. "He was just getting out of his car."

"Sorry about that. What was his name? I might know him," Killa asked, his curiosity piqued.

"Phil," Zara said, her tone heavy with sorrow.

A tension hung in the air as Killa absorbed her words. Recognition flashed in his eyes. He knew exactly who Phil was; their paths had crossed in darker times. Killa had been involved in the very circumstances that led to Phil's death, but he had never connected the dots that Phil was Zara's long-term boyfriend. "How long were y'all dating?" he inquired, though he feared the answer. "Three years," Zara replied, the pain of that lost relationship evident in her tone. Killa felt an overwhelming sense of empathy as Zara's story unfolded. "I understand why now," he said softly, his heart aching for her loss. "I'm really sorry about that." Recognizing the emotional burden she carried, he added, "It's cool though; we ain't got to do anything until you're ready." He hoped to change the subject, providing her with a sense of freedom.

Yet, Zara's resolve surprised him. "I am ready," she insisted, reaching out to him with determination. Her fingers brushed against his, signaling her willingness to bridge the gap between them, no matter how difficult theing his face and kissing him. He lifts her putting her on top of him as she takes her shirt off. He rubs his hands around her ass. He felt like he won by taking this nigga bitch now. Zara lends down kissing him as he pulled down his pants and boxers. He slightly lifts her putting his dick in. She moans leaning up. He starts bouncing her up and down seeing her hair come out of the ponytail falling. She was beautiful as hell. He was feeling her very much. He turns her over getting on top of her putting her hands over her head sticking his dick back in slow stroking her seeing her head fall back and her back bend. She felt good as fuck to him and he see why Phil was with her for 5 years. But now he needed it for his sake. Turning her over, sticking it back in, slapping her ass, cramping her until he comes all over her ass. "Damn. I see why he ain't let you go," he said, getting up.

The next morning

Zara gets up seeing Killa knocked out in her bed. She walks into the kitchen fixing breakfast for both of them. An hour later, Killa wakes up, comes to the kitchen, and sees her in a robe looking good. "I made breakfast. You just in time," she smiled, fixing his plate and seeing him come up. He wasn't thinking about breakfast in that moment, he wanted Zara for breakfast. "Yeah I'll get my second plate in a minute"

"Second plate? " Killa grabbed her waist, kissing her. "You my breakfast," he picked her up kissing her neck, and laying her back on the island. Sliding her panties off. He rubs his hands up her legs as she spreads them for him, as his tongue meets her clit. Eating her out seeing her mouth open. "Breakfast," twirling his touch around her clit, Zara grabs his head as she watches him. Kissing up her thighs, their lips met. Killa wanted Zara badly. Zara grabs his dick sticking inside herself. Feeling Killa go deep. I moan, laying back on the island as he plays with my pussy. My legs began to shake as he sped up. . "keep them up," Killa smiled, seeing her legs fall. He grabs them as he goes in and out of her. She lifts her head biting her lip as they look eye to eye. Killa pulled out giving in. He noticed Zara looking at him Dangerously. "Toxic," he giggled, putting his dick back inside his boxer.

Chapter 2

Killa left around 9. Zara gets dressed and heads to her mother's house checking up on her. She pulled up a little after twelve, seeing her car still in the driveway. She walks inside and sees her mother in the kitchen getting some Cookies out of the oven. "Ma. Do you need help? " Zara comes around the Island. Seeing her mother had it. She wasn't that damn old. "Now you know I don't need help," Debra replies. "You got some more flowers and a card this time." Referring to the roses on the counter, "Still don't have a clue where it's coming from? " Zara asked, seeing 12 dozen roses on the table with a card reading "Always will be there"

"No, I don't. But they make sure to have it delivered on time every Tuesday." Her mother was wondering the same. Every Tuesday and Friday, somebody would send Zara roses, and they never figured out who. "Weird,"

"Somebody must like you and know where I stay," Zara exchanged loving words with her mother before stepping out the door, determination in her stride. "I'll see you later. Love you," she called over her shoulder as she climbed into her car, a flurry of thoughts racing through her mind. She felt the excitement of the unknown as she typed the address of the flower shop into her GPS—today was the day she would uncover the secret behind the beautiful roses that mysteriously appeared at her home every Tuesday and Friday.

As she pulled into the parking lot of "Keep Blooming," the scent of fresh flowers wafted through the air, welcoming her inside the quaint shop. The interior was vibrant, brimming with an array of colorful blossoms, but Zara's focus remained sharp. She approached the counter, where a warm smile greeted her. "Excuse me," she began, her voice steady yet laced with curiosity. The employee looked up, her eyes sparkling with familiarity. "Yes, how can I help you?"

Zara took a breath, her heart racing. "I was trying to find out who keeps sending these beautiful roses to my address. They arrive every Tuesday and Friday, and I'm quite intrigued."

"Oh, you're Zara?" the employee replied, her tone hinting at surprise. "Yes, I am. How do you know my name?" Zara raised an eyebrow, a mix of intrigue and apprehension bubbling within her.

The employee hesitated for a moment, then continued, "Well, I'm the one who sends them to your address." She smiled, unaware that it was actually her mother's home where the roses were being delivered. Zara leaned in closer, her curiosity piqued even more. "So, do you have any idea who sends them? I'm really eager to find out." The employee shook her head gently, her expression turning apologetic. "All I know is that it's a tall, bald gentleman. He never leaves a name, unfortunately."

Zara furrowed her brow, contemplating this new information. The description didn't click into place in her mind, but it sent a shiver down her spine. "Okay, thank you. I guess you can't provide much without a name, huh?" she said, attempting to laugh off her unease. "I'm sorry I couldn't be of more help. Have a good day!" the employee said as Zara turned to leave. Stepping out into the fresh air, Zara couldn't shake the feeling of mystery that hung around the roses. Who was this man? Why was he sending flowers to her? Questions swirled in her mind as she walked away from the shop, determined to unravel the enigma of the blooms that brightened her days. Zara gets in her car, pulling off.. Phil was in a black truck watching her every move. "What now boss?"

"We gone have to send another person in to send the flowers. Other than that we can still keep an eye on her" Phil said as his driver pulled off.

3 years ago

5 days after Phil's murder. Phil slowly regained consciousness in a sterile hospital room, the beeping of machines echoing softly around him. He could feel the dull throb in his head—a constant reminder of the bullet that had nearly claimed his life. It was Blake who first

broke the silence, leaning forward with an intensity that made Phil's stomach churn. "You got shot in the head, boss. You're lucky to be alive. The bullet missed your brain by just an inch and exited cleanly," he explained, his voice grave yet filled with a hint of relief.

Phil's heart raced as he processed the news. "And Zara? My mother?" he inquired, anxiety tightening his chest. Blake's expression shifted, a shadow crossing his features. "We couldn't let them know you survived. It's complicated. We need to find out who's behind this first. You have to play dead for now. Your parents are already holding your funeral today," he explained, urgency lacing his every word.

Overwhelmed, Phil sank into the hospital bed, burying his face in his hands. "Nobody knows who did it?" he murmured, frustration and despair mixing in his voice.

Blake shook his head. "We think it's Killa—the same guy who's been gunning for your spot. When you and he were best friends, he always had a chip on his shoulder about how quickly you rose to the top."

Phil's mind raced as he absorbed this treachery. Killa, the one he once called a brother, was behind this. Anger surged through him, mixing with the pain in his head. He pushed himself upright, determination replacing his earlier despair. "Let's go," he declared, striding purposefully toward the door.

After a short drive, Phil and his bodyguards arrived at the graveyard, a place heavy with grief. He slipped out of the car and sought refuge behind a large tree, his heart aching as he gazed at the scene before him. His family was gathered, tears streaming down their faces, the weight of loss palpable in the air. Zara, especially, looked lost, as if she were fading away along with her hope.

Phil's heart twisted with guilt. He hated that he had to witness their pain from the shadows, but he knew it was necessary for now to keep them safe. He could feel the burden of his decision pressing down on him, but he forced himself to look away. Phil was a businessman owning half the clubs around Atlanta and selling houses. Killa and Phil grew up next door to each other, going into the game together just at the age of 16. When Phil was ready to get out at the age of 23, Killa wasn't with that, having them fall out about who gets what in money.

Chapter 3

3 pm

Zara pulled up to her clothing store seeing business going just how she expected it. She walks in and sees Jamie talking with a customer. Thirty minutes later. Zara stood behind the neatly organized counter of her boutique, the warm glow of the overhead lights bouncing off the light pink fabric of a tank top displayed on a nearby rack. A young woman with bright eyes and a hint of disappointment peeked at the size tag, her expression shifting as she asked, "Do you have this in an extra large?"

Zara glanced around the store, her mind racing through inventory. "We should have some in the back," she said confidently, raising her voice to call over one of her employees. "Kim!" Zara summoned, her tone a mix of urgency and command. "Can you please head to the back and restock the extra large shirts?" Turning back to the customer, Zara offered a warm, reassuring smile. "She'll be right out," she added, trying to ease the woman's disappointment.

A moment later, Jamie approached, her face etched with concern. "You good?" she asked, her voice low, clearly sensing Zara's frustration. "Yeah, just trying to figure out why the extra large tank tops weren't restocked," Zara replied, the irritation creeping into her voice.

Jamie raised an incredulous eyebrow, her dark curls bouncing slightly. "Girl, it's not there? I'll get on somebody's case about not doing their job right," she declared, her expression shifting to one of determination. Without waiting for a response, Jamie started to walk away, intent on addressing the oversight head-on. But Zara, knowing Jamie's no-nonsense approach, called her back, her expression turning serious.

"What's up, sis?" Jamie asked, turning back, a note of curiosity in her voice. Zara leaned closer, glancing around to ensure no customers were eavesdropping. "So, this random guy keeps sending roses to

Mom's house," she whispered, a mixture of humor and concern flickering across her face.

"Okay, that's totally creepy. Have you talked to Killa about it?" Jamie asked, her eyes widening, her tone shifting to one of genuine concern.

Zara let out a light laugh, shaking her head. "Why would I tell him about some guy sending me roses every Tuesday and Friday? He'd blow it way out of proportion."

"True," Jamie admitted, but her expression fell back into seriousness. "But it really is creepy. Have you looked into it?"

Zara nodded slowly. "All I know is that this tall bald guy comes in and delivers the flowers and then just leaves without saying a word."

"Does your dad know about this?" Jamie pressed, her brow furrowed with worry.

"Not at all," Zara replied, her voice tinged with disbelief and laughter. "He walks around completely oblivious to it all, treating every day like it's just another normal day."

Both women shared a chuckle, the absurdity of the situation bringing a moment of levity amidst their busy day. However, the mystery of the mysterious rose-giver lingered in the air, unresolved and strangely intriguing, as they returned to their tasks, half-heartedly keeping an eye out for any unexpected deliveries.

Zara turns around seeing Killa coming up and kissing her lips "What are you doing in here? "

"Seen you pull up. Had to come by and check on you"

"We ain't even together for you to be doing that," Zara and Killa shared a playful exchange that was filled with lighthearted banter and flirtation. As they stood close, he grinned and said, "You're mine now. Off the market," his tone mock-serious yet playful. Zara, rolling her eyes with a bright smile, playfully pushed him away and quipped back, "Oh, so I was just sitting on a shelf waiting to be picked?" Their laughter filled the air, showcasing the ease between them.

However, the mood shifted as he suggested going out to dinner. Zara's smile faltered just a bit as she explained, "I can't. My father is coming back into town." The revelation caught him by surprise, and with a quizzical look, he asked about her father's job. When she mentioned that he worked for the president, he exclaimed, "Damn, I ain't know that!" His eyes widened with an amused concern, and he asked, "Is he the type to do background checks?"

Zara chuckled, replying, "I'm the only child. Yes, I'm his baby girl." There was a warmth in her voice and a sparkle in her eye, showcasing the pride she felt in her father's dedication to her. Her friend responded with a playful grin, saying, "I ain't ready to meet Pops yet." Zara was relieved to hear him say that because she wasn't quite ready for that either. "I'm glad you said that, 'cause I ain't got time for that either," she said, her fingers lightly brushing against him, setting a playful tone for their conversation.

Later that night, Zara pulled into her driveway, the familiar sight of home wrapping around her like a warm embrace. She got out of her car and used her key to unlock the door, slipping off her shoes and leaving them by the entrance. The kitchen beckoned her with its aromas and lively atmosphere, where she found her father happily assisting his wife with dinner preparations.

"Princess," he called out affectionately, a broad smile lighting up his face as he turned to greet his daughter. Zara couldn't help but return the smile as she walked towards him, enveloping him in a warm hug. He leaned down to kiss her forehead, a simple yet meaningful gesture that spoke volumes about their close relationship. The comfort of home and the love shared between father and daughter filled the room, making the evening feel like a sweet ending to a day filled with laughter and connection.

"Heard you had roses sent every Tuesday and Friday"

"I'm already on it Dad. I don't need you to do an investigation as you call it" Zara replied

"I already figured it out," Dennis said "And the new boyfriend? He asked

"You serious right now Dad? Mom? " Zara looks at her mother, as she makes the plated.

"I can't control what your father does,"

"After what happened to Phil. I don't know if anyone is after you. So yes I will always have eyes out. But before you think he's a good guy he isn't. " he said standing with his arms folded

"And what is that supposed to mean Dad? "

"Meaning you're not the only one he's seeing. And he's a drug dealer, so with that being said don't take anything seriously"

Jamie knocks on the door. Dennis went to open it seeing her. "Ms. Green," Dennis said

"Hey Mr. Stokes," Jamie said

"Now how many times have I've told you, you don't have to call me by my last name," he said smiling "Come on in" As Jamie stepped through the door, the warm aroma of steak filled the air, greeting her senses immediately. She spotted Zara seated at the dining table, her hands resting on the polished surface. The meal was modest yet inviting, consisting of perfectly seared steak, a crisp salad, and freshly baked dinner rolls. It was a homey spread, simple but made with care.

"Hi Ms. Stokes!" Jamie exclaimed as she walked over to Zara, enveloping her in a warm hug that spoke of their close friendship. "I hope you didn't start without me," she added with a playful smile, noticing the dinner had been laid out and was eagerly awaiting them.

"Sorry, I had to go home and change," Jamie replied as she took her seat across from Zara. In a tone of genuine curiosity, she asked, "So how's the job treating your dad?"

"Fine. You know how it is—job is a job, right?" Dennis chimed in as he joined them at the table, his presence adding a familiar, comforting quality to the gathering.

Before they could truly dive into their meal, Jamie's mother interjected, "Let's say a prayer before we eat, shall we? Zara, you want to go ahead?" Zara nodded and offered a heartfelt prayer, her words echoing a gratitude for family, food, and the blessings of the day. Once the prayer concluded, they all eagerly dug into the meal, laughter and chatter filling the room.

Chapter 4

After dinner, Jamie and Zara stepped outside, their breath visible in the cool evening air as they made their way to the car. Zara's tone turned serious, and she shared troubling news. "So, Dad had the nerve to do a background check on Killa," she stated, frustration evident in her voice. "What? How does he even know?" Jamie asked, a look of disbelief on her face.

Zara sighed, running a hand through her hair. "He's got one of his guys watching me. They're probably keeping tabs on me right now."

"Wow. Well, good luck with that," Jamie offered, concern for her friend's well-being layered with anxiety about the situation.

But Zara wasn't finished. "That wasn't all. He also mentioned he's seeing someone else, and he asked me out earlier today."

"Oh hell nah!" Jamie exclaimed, her eyes widening in indignation. "I'm with your dad on this one. That's just wrong." Once they returned to the house, the atmosphere shifted as Dennis summoned his wife for a serious discussion. "So we need to talk," he began, a weight in his tone suggesting the gravity of what was to come.

"What is it, honey?" she replied, sensing the tension.

Dennis paused, looking contemplative before he finally spoke. "Phil is alive..." The words hung in the air, thick with unspoken implications and a shocking revelation that would undoubtedly change everything.

"WHAT? HOW? " she said as she stopped washing dishes.

"He's the one who been sending the roses. I ain't talk to him yet. Matter of fact he doesn't know I know"

"Zara gone flip if she finds out. Why you ain't tell her? "

"I don't know his motive yet. I'm figuring that out now" Dennis was gone find his motive and why he been a ghost for all these years "He got shot in the head"

"He survived. That's why we couldn't see the body. The bullet came out. " Dennis continues to explain

"Are you going find and talk to him? "

"Already on it. Just don't say nothing to Zara about it" Dennis said

Zara pulled up to her house and saw Killa's car parked there. She gets out seeing him get out too. "Hey baby," he said coming to hug her.

"Hey," she said as he tried to kiss her, but she pulled away waking up to the house. As they entered the dimly lit living room of Zara's house, an air of tension settled between them. The walls, adorned with framed memories of laughter and joy, seemed to witness the unspoken conflict brewing. Zara crossed her arms, a defensive posture that betrayed her heightened emotions. "So, who else are you messing with?" she demanded, locking her gaze onto him, her voice steady yet edged with intensity.

His confusion was palpable; he stammered, "What?" The surprise in his eyes only intensified her resolve. "You heard me," she reiterated, her tone leaving no room for evasion. "And before you answer, it better be what I want to hear, not what I don't want to hear." She paced slightly, the energy in the room thickening as he hesitated.

With a reluctant sigh, he replied, "Just a chick from the block, that's it." His admission hung heavily between them, laden with implications. Zara's expression hardened. "So us, this... it ain't gonna work out," she stated matter-of-factly, a bittersweet finality lacing her words.

"I stopped messing with her," he blurted, desperation creeping into his voice.

"What today?" Zara shot back, her brow arched. The silence that followed was deafening, filled with unacknowledged truths.

"Look," she finally said, breaking the quiet with a tone of resolution. "We can't do this. I don't need any drama in my life. So whatever you have going on is on you. We can be cool, but that's it."

Her words struck a chord, and he couldn't help but ask, "Wait. How did you find out? Are you watching me?"

Zara let out a soft laugh, dismissing his concern. "I don't need to watch you," she replied, a hint of amusement mingling with her frustration. "I know we're starting to get in a good place, but you need to understand, it's you I want."

With a determined glint in her eye, Zara challenged him, "Then prove it." Without missing a beat, he pulled out his phone, ostensibly ready to make a serious commitment. "You ain't got to ask twice," he said, but Zara interrupted him. "Nah. Speaker!" she asserted, pointing a finger with authority.

The tension in the room heightened as the girl on the other end answered with a bright, unsuspecting greeting. "Hello, baby," she chirped, oblivious to the impending confrontation. Zara's arms folded tighter across her chest, a metaphorical barrier between past and present.

"Aye, look," he started, his voice laced with urgency. "We ain't gonna work out." A ripple of anger surged from the phone. "For what?" the girl demanded, her tone rising sharply. "You cutting me off?"

"Yeah, man. Can't do this," he affirmed, staring at Zara, knowing this moment might define their future. As the conversation unfolded, it became clear that both women were wrestling with their emotions, caught in a web of unreciprocated feelings and unresolved tensions. Zara stood firm, her heart racing, fully aware that this was a critical juncture in their complicated relationship.

"Kill.... " He hangs up

Zara sees him on his phone. She snatches it going to the same bitch number, he just called. "What are you doing? "

"Blocking her," he said showing her.

"Hit delete too," she said and he did just that.

"Anything else? " he asked "First how do you know? "

"My father," she said walking away into the kitchen.

"How the fuck he know?" Amidst a tense conversation, a Killa grapples with his unease about being watched, specifically by Zara's father, a powerful figure who works closely with the president. His anxiety is palpable as he confides in Zara, seeking reassurance. However, Zara finds humor in his worries, her laughter echoing in stark contrast to his serious tone. "Scared?" she teases, poking fun at his concerns. The young man, visibly affected by the implications of her father's position, responds earnestly, "Yeah, a little. I can't lie about that."

Outside Zara's house, the atmosphere shifts dramatically as Dennis strides toward a black truck, flanked by three of his associates. With a commanding presence, they approach the vehicle and forcefully open the doors, disarming its occupants before they can react. "Phil," Dennis calls out, his hands tucked casually into his pockets, projecting an air of confidence and control.

Phil, recognizing Dennis, meets his gaze with a mix of surprise and apprehension. "Mr. Stokes," he replies, trying to maintain his composure. "How did you find me?"

Dennis smirks slightly, knowing he always keeps a watchful eye on the people he cares about. "You should know already. Nothing slips past me, even when I'm far away. Let's talk." As they both climb into Dennis's sleek black truck, the engine roars to life and they take off into the night, leaving the chaos behind.

Inside the vehicle, the tension remains palpable. "What's happening?" Dennis inquires, his voice steady and focused.

"Still trying to figure out who tried to kill me," Phil responds, the weight of his words hanging heavily in the air. Dennis arches an eyebrow, skepticism clear in his expression. "So, you thought the best plan was to disappear for three years?" Phil's frustration simmers beneath the surface. "Had to do what I had to do, as a man. Ain't have a choice," Dennis wanted to know who did and what his plan was. "You know who did it?"

Phil looks over at Dennis. "Nah, Mr. Stokes. Think it's somebody close to me. And the only nigga I was close with, was this nigga names Killa,"

Dennis was taking back by the name. "The same nigga my daughter seeing?" Dennis instantly asked, seeing if Phil already knew. "That's who she seeing?" confused himself. He comes to think about was this Killas plan all alone. They both was left shocked and confused.

Chapter 5

Three months had drifted by since the tense exchange between Dennis and his partner, which had left them both on edge. They had speculated about a potential threat surrounding Zara, suspecting that someone close to her might be involved in a way they hadn't yet figured out. The name Killa lingered in Dennis's mind, a man he had concerns about, especially since Zara had become attached to him in such a short amount of time.

Dennis kept a vigilant watch over Zara, ensuring that his team was constantly on standby, ready to step in if anything seemed amiss. Phil, too, was wrapped up in the surveillance, keenly aware of the delicate situation. Meanwhile, Zara had seemingly moved deeper into her relationship with Killa. Today, as she pulled into the driveway of Killa's modest home, she felt a flutter of excitement.

Zara stepped out of her car, her heart racing as she approached the front door. Killa opened it almost instantly, a wide grin spreading across his face. "Sup, baby," he greeted her, leaning down to plant a soft kiss on her lips. In that moment, all her worries evaporated; Killa had been treating her with genuine care, surprising her with romantic dates and thoughtful gifts that made her feel cherished.

"Hey," she replied, her voice light and cheerful. "You ready?"

"Yeah, let's go," Killa said, a spark of enthusiasm in his eyes as he reached for his car keys. They slid into his vehicle, the engine purring to life, and Killa pulled out into the street, excitement buzzing in the air between them. As they drove off, they were oblivious to the watchful eyes that monitored their every move, unaware that their freedom came bundled with the complexities of past connections that still loomed in the shadows. Zara wanted to go out for dinner but somewhere chill too. "Kind of want to go somewhere different. Like an R&B lounge. Are you okay with that? " Zara asked

"Never been. But I'm down"

Zara puts in the address as he heads on the highway. They pulled up to the R&B lounge within 29 minutes. They walked in looking around. "Hey Zara," a girl said walking passed her.

"Well known in here" Killa asked seeing people wave at Zara.

"I know a few people," She said. They walked to a section. "So, sit down I'll give somebody to bring you a drink"

"And where you going? " Killa grabs her hand

"You'll see," She kissed him, walking off as people started talking to her.

A lady looks up to Killa "What can I get you tonight? "

"Got some apple crown?" he points as she shook her head and walked away. At an energetic event, the crowd buzzed with anticipation as a dark-skinned man took to the stage, microphone in hand. "How's everybody tonight?" he asked, radiating enthusiasm and pointing to the audience, who responded with cheers. He introduced the main act with excitement, saying, "Welcome Zara y'all!" The atmosphere in the room shifted, with some nearby patrons, including Killa, whispering about Zara's impressive singing ability.

When Zara stepped onto the stage, she greeted the audience with a wave and a bright smile. "So tonight I decided to sing Beyoncé's '1+1,' and I know y'all will like it," she announced. As the music began, she closed her eyes, took a deep breath, and immersed herself in the performance. Killa, caught off guard by her talent, stood up and moved closer to the stage, captivated by her presence. As her voice soared through the venue, the audience was mesmerized.

When the performance concluded, applause erupted, and Killa impulsively lifted Zara off the stage in an exuberant celebration of her talent. "Damn, I didn't know you could blow like that," he exclaimed, beaming with admiration. Zara, feeling accomplished, replied playfully, "Just wanted to surprise you," before sharing a tender kiss with him. Their connection deepened as she glanced up at him, momentarily lost in the moment. And when Zara opened her eyes, a face was standing in the distance with a black suit on. Killa grabs her face making her look at him. But, she hurried up and looked back thinking she just saw Phil. "You good? " Killa asked looking behind him.

"Yeah, I'm fine," Zara said still looking. She could have sworn, she saw Phil.

Phil got in his black truck putting his hands on his head. He loved Zara with everything in him. And seeing her have a love for his ex-best friend was starting to tear him apart.

An hour later

Killa holding Zara in the air kissing as they enter his house. Walking past the living room to his bedroom. Killa slams his door putting Zara down and undoing her dress. He takes his pants and boxers off, picks her back up, and puts her on his bed. They made love putting Zara right out.

An hour later

Killa was in the kitchen with his boys smoking a blunt. Zara gets up 30 minutes later thirsty. She gets out of bed opening the door. She hears Killa talking to his guys.

"Damn bruh I ain't know that," his homebody said "She doesn't know you killed Phil? " he asked

"Hell nah she doesn't know. And keep your voice down nigga," Killa hit the blunt, shaking his head at the same time. Zara heard what Killa said becoming scared. "Look, I do love her, though. It ain't no get back. But what she doesn't know is the best. Long she doesn't find out we coo. If she does, then I don't know what to do." Zara tip-toed back into Killa's bedroom, shutting the door. She got back in his bed scared for her life. "What the fuck" is all Zara was thinking in her head. She was scared and afraid.

Chapter 6

The next morning

Zara was looking at Killa sound asleep right in her face. She rubs him thinking about what he said last night. If he was the one she needed to tell her father. But she wouldn't also know what would happen to her if Killa found out she overheard him. Her phone rings just in time. She got up to answer it. "Hello"

"hey, Got time to come into the shop? " Jamie asked

"Yeah, I'll be there," Zara said feeling so much relief.

Killa gets up rubbing his eyes "Leaving? " seeing her grabbed her purse and keys off his dresser.

"Yeah, Jamie needs me at the shop. I'll text you" Zara said walking to his door.

He gets up. "Damn a nigga cant get a kiss" Zara gave him a kiss and left Killa house. She drove home to shower and change, eventually arriving at her shop two hours later.

Once inside, she immediately pulled her friend Jamie into the back office, her face serious. "Okay, you good?" Jamie asked as Zara closed the door. Zara began pacing, revealing her concern. "I overheard Killa say he killed Phil," she announced, her voice tense.

Jamie was shocked. "Bitch, WHAT? Are you sure?" she responded.

Zara affirmed that she wasn't mistaken, having overheard Killa's conversation with his friends. "You need to stay away from him," Jamie urged.

"I can't," Zara replied, anxiety creeping into her voice. "Killa might find out that I'm hiding something. Everything is going well between us, and if he discovers that I know... he said he wouldn't know what to do with me. That scares me."

"Tell pops. Seriously. You need to do it now. He's dangerous," Jamie insisted.

"Easy for you to say," Zara shot back.

Jamie, who had known Killa and Phil, from back in the day. Jamie never knew they was even friends or done things together growing up. She just knew them from school. But she knew their dangerous tendencies all too well but was relieved that Phil had changed his ways. The weight of the situation hung heavy as Zara wrestled with her fear and uncertainty. "Look if you start feeling unsafe tell your dad. I'm serious. Or I will"

"Not now though Jamie"

"I'll give it time," she said "Going out tonight? "

"Yes. Much needed"

"Well let's knock this day the fuck out," Jamie said as they laughed.

9 pm.

Jamie bedroom

Zara had on a burgundy dress that went a little passed her knees. Her boobs poked out sitting up just right without a bra. Jamie stood in front of her full-length mirror, her long, luxurious hair cascading down her back in stunning waves—30 inches of rich, dark locks. She slipped into a figure-hugging white dress that flirted just above her curves, perfectly complementing her stylish white open-toed heels. Her look was completed with perfectly styled curls that framed her face, enhancing her radiant smile.

"Ready?" Jamie asked, her eyes sparkling with anticipation.

"Let's go," Zara replied, beaming as they stepped out of Jamie's cozy bedroom, their laughter echoing down the hall.

As they arrived at the club, the bass from the music pulsed through the air. The two friends exited the car and confidently strode inside after presenting their IDs at the entrance. The atmosphere inside was lively but not overwhelming; the crowd was just the right size, busy enough to feel exciting but not so packed that they felt lost in the throngs of people.

"Decent," Zara remarked, scanning the room as they made their way toward the bar, where the dim lighting and vibrant décor set the perfect backdrop for their girls' night out.

"Let's hope it stays this way. It usually gets crazy after 11," Jamie replied, her voice slightly laced with apprehension as she thought back to past nights that had turned chaotic.

They ordered shots of vodka and raised their glasses in a toast before heading to the dance floor. The rhythmic music filled their bodies with energy as they began to dance, letting loose and enjoying each other's company. Their friendship, forged in the halls of middle school, had only grown stronger over the years. Jamie's early life had been a struggle; with neglectful parents caught in the throes of addiction, it was Zara's family that had stepped in, treating Jamie like one of their own, providing the support she desperately needed.

About an hour later, the atmosphere shifted as Killa entered the club. He was flanked by several of his friends, his presence commanding attention as he navigated through the crowd with confidence. When he spotted Zara on the dance floor, her laughter ringing out like music, he couldn't resist approaching her. He crept up from behind, a mischievous smile playing on his lips.

"Ain't heard from you all day," he said, his voice low and teasing as he wrapped his arms around her waist, leaning in close to speak in her ear.

Zara, momentarily taken by surprise, turned around to face him, her heart racing. She feigned nonchalance, attempting to keep her cool despite the fluttering in her chest that Killa's presence always seemed to incite. The energy in the club surged around them as the night unfolded, the potential for adventure hovering in the air. happened. She smiled "Sorry we've been busy"

"Busy? " He said looking around "could have told me you were coming to the club"

"Again, I'm sorry," She said still smiling and kissing him.

"Going home with me tonight? " he asked

"I can't. Jamie wanted me to come over to her house. We have designs that need to be run over. Right, Jamie," as she grabs her shoulder, pushing her aside of her.

"Yeah, yeah. We do. So she not available tonight or tomorrow." Jamie smiled, looking at Killa, who they knew was no goofy.

"Y'all good? How much y'all been drinking tonight? " he asked seeing them acting weird.

"Maybe we took too many shots," Jamie laughed.

"We'll since we here. We can spend a few more hours together" Killa grabbed her hand as they started dancing. Zara kept looking into the eyes knowing he killed her lover.

Chapter 7

6 years ago. Phil stepped into the modest apartment he shared with Killa, a cozy yet cluttered space that reflected their contrasting personalities. Phil was meticulous, someone who took pride in keeping their living environment neat and orderly. In stark contrast, Killa had a reputation for being disorganized, often leaving a trail of chaos in his wake.

Phil dropped a well-worn duffle bag onto the small kitchen table with a heavy thud. As the bag opened, stacks of cash tumbled out, glistening like trophies from their risky endeavors. Killa, drawn by the rustling sound, peeked around the corner, his eyes widening with surprise. "Damn! This how much you made in a day?" he remarked, quickly scooping up the cash with a mix of admiration and disbelief.

"Hell yeah," Phil replied, a sense of pride in his tone.

Killa fished through the stacks and calculated the bounty before him. "This is over $100,000," he exclaimed, setting the money down on the table with a thud that emphasized its weight.

Sitting down beside Killa, Phil shifted the conversation to his future. "I've been thinking... I want to get out of the game. Start my own business," he said, his voice steady as he outlined his vision for a different life—one filled with potential and prosperity, far removed from the shadows of their current activities.

Killa scoffed at the idea, shaking his head. "Hell nah. Not right now," he shot back, his tone resolute. He was firmly entrenched in the life they led, reveling in the lucrative nature of their illicit dealings.

"Shawn, I ain't planning on staying in this shit forever," Phil countered, frustration creeping into his voice. He believed in their bond and thought they could venture into a new chapter together. "We came up in the game together, man. I just want to build something solid for us."

But Killa's determination to stick to what they knew remained unyielding. "Bro, you're thinking too far ahead," he replied, dismissing Phil's dreams as naïve. Despite Phil's hopeful intentions, Killa felt anchored to their current life, convinced that they could continue thriving within the boundaries of their dangerous world. Their conflicting visions for the future hung heavy in the air, hinting at the rift that would eventually change everything. "Look, whatever you gone do. Do it. We gone count this cash, separate it, and figure the rest of this shit out. And you should come with me"

"I ain't going to college. Fuck that. Too good for school"

"It's not all about being street smart. Book smart too. But I'm not gone tell you what to do. Just don't let this shit get in between us. We boys and I'm never gone leave you out. "

"Yeah, whatever nigga." Killa said "You moving out too? "

"yeah nigga" he said laughing. "Look I'm still going be around. Just at school mostly." Phil gets up and walks up to Killa, shaking up with him. "We boys"

"Boys," Killa said lighting his blunt again "Look I'll handle the last drop tonight while you sort out the money"

"Cool," Phil said going to his room. Killa watched him as he walked into his room. He grabbed his phone out of his pocket calling one of his homeboys.

Later that day. Killa pulled up to his homeboy crib getting out and knocking on the door. Trent opened the door. "Sup nigga? " Trent said

"Man, this nigga talking about getting out the game," he walked in and went into the living room, sitting down.

"What?" Trent closed the door seeing Killa walk straight past him. "Yeah, man. Talking about him going to college to get a real job. " Killa was feeling some type of way. He and Phil built this shit just for him to go. "He damn near built this shit," Trent and Killa were deep in conversation, their minds racing with confusion and frustration over their friend Phil's unexpected desire to step away from their way of life. Killa shook his head, incredulous that Phil hadn't approached him sooner with his thoughts. The bond they shared felt threatened, and Killa couldn't shake the feeling of betrayal. "What are you planning to do about it?" Trent asked, his brow furrowed with concern.

Killa's expression hardened with resolve. "I'm not leaving the game. I've made too much money to just walk away now." He leaned back slightly, trying to gather his thoughts. The weight of their situation pressed heavily upon them. Both men couldn't believe that Phil would abandon the life they had built together. Trent, frustrated, remarked, "If you're out of the game, you're out for good. There's no coming back halfway."

Killa nodded in agreement, feeling the same urgency. "Exactly. Let go. "

Later that day Killa walks in seeing Phil packing the rest of his stuff. He was mad and wanted to let his boy know how he felt about his decision. "Look, I don't like that you choose to leave the game. And not talk about this sit months before. And I know you knew before a head of time that you been made you choice?" Killa explain seeing Phil look up at him.

"Nigga I'm trying to have a better life. I didn't say, I was out the game. Nigga I'm trying to make the game better. Move sit from city to city not just here in the Atl. What is you thinking nigga?" Phil becomes angry with how his boy acting. He never expects him to feel a type of way for going for something better. Killa walks into Phil's face. "You heard me. You know how it goes," Killa said as they stood face to face.

"You mad a nigga choosing a different route? "

"Nigga you a bailout"

"Wow! Same old nigga. Keep that petty money. You know I got way more than that," Phil said, walking into his room, grabbing all his cash, and packing a duffle bag full of clothes. He doesn't need Killa at all. Killa always needed him.

Chapter 8

Two weeks later

Killa and Phil fell out not speaking. Phil moved all his stuff out moving into his apartment close to the college. It was his first day. He dropped the cash for the rest of the school year to attend. Everything was paid for. Phil arrived at Georgia State University, parking his BMW and grabbing his backpack before stepping onto campus. Despite being unfamiliar with anyone there, he was comfortable in his solitude. As he walked, a group of laughing girls passed by, and one of them accidentally bumped into him. "Sorry," she said, turning to him.

"Good morning beautiful. I'm Phil," he replied, captivated by her. The girl introduced herself as Zara, flashing a smile as they shook hands. Phil noticed Jamie, another girl from the group, who recognized him right away.

"Wait, Phil? You don't seem like a college type," Jamie remarked, her laughter filling the air.

"Y'all know each other?" Zara asked, looking between them.

Phil replied, "Go way back," but his attention remained fixed on Zara, who caught his eye with her beauty.

Jamie continued with a teasing tone, "What are you doing in college? Kind of late in the semester, don't you think?"

"Jamie," Zara chimed in, chuckling at the comment.

"Just being nosey," Jamie defended herself, but Phil simply shrugged off the question.

"Yeah, I know. But, it's never too late to do what you need to do. It was nice to see you again Jamie and nice to see you Zara," Phil began to walk backward still staring at Zara before turning around, going about his day. Despite being late to the semester, he was determined to make the most of his time there. As he walked away, he felt a sense of excitement; he was ready to pursue something new for the first time, rather than waiting to be chased. "Now who's that,? " Zara asked

"Well, Phil obviously. But I grew up around him. We went to school together, before your parents let me move in with y'all. But he was a drug dealer. He and this dude named Shawn always made stacks by just walking around the block. So I'm shocked he's here"

"Yeah my dad ain't going," Zara said laughing and walking off.

30 minutes later Phil was already sitting in Sociology class. He sees Zara walk in with another female. She smiles seeing Phil with his pen in his hands. As the class filled up Zara and Phil couldn't help but keep looking at each other.

"Good morning Class," Mrs. Odom said coming in and sitting her things down. "So let's talk Sociology," she said smiling and walking around from her desk.

As class began Zara and Phil couldn't help but to keep looking at each other. It was an undeniable spark ignited between Zara and Phil from the moment their paths crossed. After class, Zara stepped out into the bustling hallway, her mind still buzzing with lecture notes when she noticed Phil standing by the entrance, looking somewhat lost and uncertain about where to head next for his next class. Intrigued, she approached him with a friendly smile and asked, "Need help?"

Phil looked up, flashing a charming grin that lit up his handsome features, and replied, "Just a little." He watched her with keen interest as she playfully grabbed the schedule paper from his hands, glancing over the courses he was taking.

"Business management, huh?" Zara said, raising an eyebrow and meeting his gaze with a teasing smile. "Interesting choice."

"Yeah," Phil responded, his confidence shining through as he acknowledged her presence. "I'm trying to become a businessman. Is there something wrong with that?"

She chuckled lightly, leaning against the wall as they started walking together through the crowded hallway. "Not at all. You just don't really seem like the type."

Amused, Phil shot her a sidelong glance. "What's my type then?"

With a playful laugh, Zara replied, "Definitely not the typical college student."

Phil joined in her laughter, then mused aloud, "Maybe I need to explore a different path. But don't let my laid-back look fool you; I'm smart as hell. You'd be surprised."

"I love surprises," Zara said, her curiosity piqued.

"I can tell," he teased, enjoying their back-and-forth. Zara playfully protested, "Don't start reading me too much," giggling at their banter.

With a sudden burst of confidence, Phil said, "How about I take you to lunch? I'd like to get to know you better."

Zara paused for a moment, caught off guard by his directness. "Just going right for it, huh?"

"Why wait?" he replied, his tone earnest and inviting.

"And if I say no?" she countered, her smile playing coyly on her lips.

Phil shrugged, a confident grin still plastered on his face. "Then I'll accept it as a man. At least I tried," he said, exuding a mix of charm and sincerity.

Zara raised an eyebrow, intrigued by his casual attitude. "Oh, so you're not going to get mad or anything?"

"Why should I?" he said with a lighthearted chuckle. "Because I want to get to know you, right? If you're not interested, that's okay. But I think we could have a lot of fun together."

As they continued their conversation, the chemistry between them deepened, marked by laughter and flirtation, as the hallway around them faded into the background. "And im not the type to get mad fast. Specially not over small shit like that. I'm cool"

"Then I'd like lunch then," she said as she stopped in front of his class handing him back his paper. "This me? " He asked.

"Yup. This you? " Zara replied. Phil grabbed her notebook opening it putting his number inside. "Hope to see you text me. Don't ghost me" he smiled grabbing her chin walking into class. Zara smiles as she walked away.

Chapter 9

Zara walks out of class with Jamie heading out of the building. "Glad that's over," Zara said

"Girl, hate I have to take that fucking class. But we have to do what we have to do," Jamie said as they giggled. "Lunch?"

"Now you know my ass have to go to work in that boring ass library," Zara said as they both walked towards they dorm room. An hour later. Zara stood tall and resolute as she confronted her friend Jamie outside the campus library. "I don't see why you're even working," Jamie exclaimed, a hint of disbelief in her voice. "Your dad promised to pay for both of us."

Zara shook her head firmly, her expression one of determination. "No disrespect, Jamie, but I refuse to live off his or my mother's money. I need to earn my own way," she replied, taking a step back with her books cradled protectively against her chest. There was pride in her voice; she had been raised with a strong work ethic and knew the value of self-sufficiency.

"Don't forget we have that frat party to go to tonight!" Jamie called after her, trying to redirect Zara's thoughts to a more carefree subject.

Zara abruptly froze, lightning-fast realization dawning on her. "DAMN, I FORGOT!" she shouted, her face lighting up with excitement.

"NO, THE FUCK YOU DIDN'T!" Jamie responded, her tone playful yet incredulous.

Just then, a teacher walked by, overhearing the commotion. "Ms. Jones, language!" the teacher interjected, a mix of authority and amusement in her voice.

Zara couldn't help but laugh at the situation, flashing a cheeky smile at Jamie as she playfully blew her friend a kiss before turning away. She headed to work, her mind buzzing with mixed feelings of responsibility and the thrill of the evening ahead.

Hours later, Zara found herself in the bookstore, moving along the aisles and meticulously returning misplaced volumes to their proper spots. Each book was a reminder of the world of knowledge she adored, yet today her heart wasn't in it. Despite the comfortable upbringing she had enjoyed as an only child, where everything she desired was handed to her without the need to lift a finger, the weight of adulthood pressed on her shoulders. Now, at 18, she was adamant about embracing true independence. With her father's financial safety net beneath her, she felt a fierce craving for freedom and wanted to explore the experience of making her own money. Living the adult life was her goal, and she was determined to seize it wholeheartedly.

Zara feels a tap on her shoulder. She turns around seeing Phil standing in front of her. His hands was up by his chest with his fingers wrapped around his strap, holding on to his backpack. He looks down at Zara smelling just like Prada. His dreads was nicely done. The tattoo on his neck was noticeable which Zara liked it.

"Phil, right?" She smiles and asked

"Zara," he tilts his head side way smiling at her. "

"Need help? Or you looking for something specifically?" She asked, holding some books in her hand.

"Came to see if I can get my assigned books," he replies, not letting his eyes off her.

"They was suppose to been give to you when you came," In the hushed ambiance of the library, where dust motes danced lazily in beams of soft sunlight filtering through tall windows, Zara felt a sudden surge of clumsiness. She lost her grip on a stack of thick, well-worn books, watching helplessly as they tumbled to the polished wooden floor with a dull thud. The quiet stir of the library was briefly interrupted, drawing the attention of Phil, who was nearby. He quickly knelt down, his presence steady and reassuring, as he began to help her gather the scattered volumes.

As they stood up together, the world around them seemed to fade away, leaving only the charged air between them. Their eyes locked, and Zara felt her pulse quicken, an exhilarating mix of embarrassment and intrigue washing over her. She was acutely aware of the heat radiating from her cheeks, her heart pounding as Phil held her gaze with an intensity that made her breath hitch.

"You going to tell me where to go, or will you show me?" he asked playfully, his voice smooth and teasing. He stepped slightly closer, creating an electric tension that made Zara acutely aware of his proximity. She could feel her palms grow clammy, and the air felt thick between them, inviting yet daunting.

Swallowing hard, she averted her gaze, desperately trying to regain her composure. "Um, yeah, I'll just get you a map for the college," she managed to say, her voice barely a whisper. With a deep breath, she turned and walked toward the front desk, each step feeling heavy with the weight of his lingering attention.

As she moved, Zara noticed Phil's eyes on her, a mixture of admiration and curiosity in his expression. She found herself acutely aware of her own reflection in his gaze: the way her naturally curly black hair framed her face, mirroring her untamed spirit, and how the sunlight made her skin glow with a warm, golden hue. Her fitted clothes accentuated her curves, and each step felt like a dance.

Phil's attraction to Zara deepened with every passing moment, his heart racing as he fought to contain his desire. Biting his lip, he followed her movements, intrigued by her elegance and confidence, eager to learn more about the girl who had so effortlessly captured his attention. As Zara returned with the map, he couldn't help but maintain a playful demeanor, his heart thumping with the thrill of their newfound connection, the unspoken chemistry hanging between them like a delicate thread waiting to be pulled.

Zara reaches over the desk while looking at Phil. She grabs these small maps, that were giving out to the college just in case anyone needs them.

"Here you go. This will tell you everything you need to know," she said, reaching out her hand.

"And would if I want to get to know you?" He asked

Zara smiles, putting her head down. She felt a flutter of nerves mixed with unexpected excitement as Phil sauntered over to her, flashing a charming smile that showcased his impressively white teeth. His easy confidence drew her in, and when he nonchalantly suggested they go out for dinner, her heart skipped a beat. She hesitated, the word "maybe" escaping her lips, a soft veil over her true feelings.

Phil raised his eyebrows playfully, tilting his head slightly, clearly intrigued. "Maybe?" he echoed, a hint of challenge in his tone.

"Yeah, maybe," she replied, a shy smile breaking through.

With an intensity that made her pulse quicken, he leaned closer, insisting, "I needs that maybe to be a yes. Just dinner then. And you can't say you feeling me." Standing tall and looking particularly good in the dim lighting, he exuded an easy charm that made it hard for her to resist.

"Maybe," Zara said again, feeling increasingly drawn to him as he took a small step closer.

Just then, Mrs. Lisa's voice cut through their moment. "Ms. Mason," she called from her office, her tone laced with curiosity.

Zara turned, slightly flustered. "Yes, Mrs. Mason?" she responded, her heart racing.

"Is everything okay? Trouble finding something?" Mrs. Lisa asked, her demeanor suggesting she might be a bit too invested in their conversation.

Zara quickly regained her composure. "Everything is fine. He was just lost," she said, casting a quick glance back at Phil, who stood by, looking amused. Leaning in, she whispered to him, "Just lunch?"

"Just dinner," he said firmly, a playful grin on his face, unfazed by her shift.

"Okay, I'll be off at 8," she replied, feeling a mix of anticipation and excitement. "Now get out of here. She's just being nosey." With that, she watched Phil stroll away, a lingering smile on her lips.

As the clock neared 8 PM, Phil made his way back to the library, the evening settling into a peaceful stillness around him. The fading light cast shadows across the room, and he spotted Zara by the desk, reaching over to gather her belongings. He paused at the door, watching her with a mix of admiration and eagerness until she finally turned around.

"Fuck!" Zara exclaimed, her eyes wide with surprise as she caught sight of him. The unexpected jolt of their encounter set the stage for an evening filled with promise and potential, the air thick with unspoken words and lingering glances. "Phil, you scared the fuck out of me," she whispers seeing him coming up smiling.

"Shit, my bad. I thought I wouldn't scare you standing by the door?" Zara lingered by the door, her heart racing slightly as anticipation bubbled within her. Phil stands with a relaxed smile, the kind that made her feel at ease amidst the chaos of the surroundings. "You ready?" he asked, his eyes glimmering with excitement.

"Yeah, but I have to go change first," she replied, glancing down at her casual attire. They walked out of the library together, the scent of old books still lingering in the air as they navigated the busy hallways. Zara couldn't help but notice the sea of faces around her—some were familiar, casual acquaintances from her past on the step team, while others were strangers, faces she recognized only in passing.

As they strolled, Amber, one of her closest friends, spotted her and quickly made her way over, a playful expression on her face. "Hey, Zara! Are you going to the frat party tonight?" she asked, her eyes sparkling with enthusiasm.

Zara shook her head, a small smile tugging at her lips. "No, I didn't plan on it."

"Why not? You know you'd be the face of the party!" Amber exclaimed, making a mock puppy dog face that was hard to resist.

Zara chuckled softly. "And that's exactly why I'm not going, Amber. Bye!" She waved her off while still smiling, feeling a mixture of affection and exasperation for her friend.

Phil looked at her, eyebrows raised in surprise. "Face of the party?" he inquired, tilting his head slightly. Zara shrugged, trying to keep things light. "Ehh, I hate being the center of attention. That's one of the reasons I don't go," she admitted as they hopped into the elevator, the doors sliding shut with a soft thud.

As they exited the elevator and made their way down the corridor to her dorm room, Zara unlocked the door and stepped inside. The familiar scent of their living space greeted her, but it was Jamie, her roommate, who caught her attention. Jamie was already dressed for the party, her outfit vibrant and eye-catching—a stark contrast to Zara's comfortable, laid-back style.

"What are you doing here?" Jamie asked Phil with an inquisitive glance, her hands on her hips.

"Just taking Zara out for dinner," Phil replied, his tone casual yet purposeful.

Zara sensed the warmth of their friendship enveloping her, but she was also acutely aware of the choices that lay ahead. As she prepared to change and head out with Phil, she couldn't shake the feeling that tonight would be a turning point, a moment where she would have to confront her own fears and desires within the backdrop of friendship and fleeting adventures. " Don't think you slick," Jamie looks at Zara going over to the closet and getting something out to wear.

"I told you, I ain't want to go to that damn party," Zara began to laugh feeling relief come off her body. She ain't wat the attention and never like it.

"So what? Go by myself?" Jamie asked

"Know damn well. You are meeting Amber and them there. Speaking of them, they on their way there now," she said

"Ohhh," Jamie hurried and grabbed her purse. "This conversation ain't over, and Phil. That's my bestie. Chop your dick off and feed it to the birds if you do something to her," she said, walking out.

"Ouch!" Phil watches as Jamie left out.

Chapter 10

Phil sits across from Zara, watching her grab a Buffalo boneless wing with her fork sticking it in her mouth. Zara covers her mouth, seeing Phil look over at her. "What? I have something on me?" She asked as he laughed, shaking his head no.

"Tell me something. You seem like a good girl, with probably a good family behind you," He asked, crossing his fingers together, sitting them on the table in front of him..

Zara smiles. "My dad, he's work for the president. My mom a laywer," As Zara savored another bite of her perfectly seasoned chicken, she glanced over at Phil, who was munching on a fry. Their conversation flowed comfortably, and she found herself genuinely curious about his story. "So, what's a girl like you doing here? Why not Spelman?" Phil asked, a hint of intrigue in his voice.

Zara smiled softly, reflecting on her choice. "I wanted to be here, close to my mom. I just didn't see myself leaving my hometown so soon," she replied, her eyes momentarily drifting as she thought about her family.

Phil pondered her response, giving a small nod as he changed the subject. "Hmm. So, what about you? Why start the semester so late?" He took a sip of his drink, studying her expression.

Zara grabbed a fry, her curiosity piqued even further. "Needed a different route in my life," he confessed, his tone growing more serious as he spoke.

Intrigued, she leaned in. "And what was the life you had before coming here?" she asked, her voice gentle yet probing.

"If you don't judge, I don't mind telling," Phil replied, his desire for honesty evident in his eyes.

Zara nodded earnestly. "I won't judge you."

With a deep breath, he opened up. "I used to be in the streets. The money was good—better than I ever thought possible—but you know, doing that every day got tiring. My pops always told me I'd be a smart man, but I chose the streets anyway," Phil said, his gaze dropping to the table as he spoke, as if he were reliving the weight of those choices.

Zara stopped eating, processing his words. "You can speak your mind," he encouraged her, looking back up to gauge her reaction.

"Well," she started carefully, "I've never messed with a street dude. I'm not saying it's bad; I just wouldn't want to put my life in the hands of someone who already has a dangerous lifestyle, if that makes sense." Her voice was steady, but there was an underlying tension as she laid out her feelings.

"I get you," Phil said, his expression reflective as he absorbed her perspective.

Zara smiled softly, wanting to support him despite their differing paths. "But I'm really glad you chose to change for the better. It's never too late to turn things around, right?" she added, her encouragement hanging in the air, filled with the hope of new beginnings. Phil looks up, smiling, showing his pretty teeth. He knew Zara was not gone fuck with him, but he knows he still have a chance to change her mind about him.

"What's your type of dude?" He asked

"I like a man who's soft, responsible, respectful, got something going for themselves. A man who's provides, protects, and leads. That's what I'm trying to say," Zara said, laughing. "But it seems like I've tried the perfect guy stage. And it's not working,"

"Got a whole book of shit. Huh?" Phil laughed

"Okay, now that I think about it. I just want a partner. Just someone to love me the right way," she said. "What about you?"

Phil smiles. "Let me just say, I've never had a good girl. The type of girls I've always ran into was the crazy one. Always ready to fight. And nothing going for themselves. And when In the streets themselves. In a charming, softly lit restaurant, the aroma of delicious food filled the air as Zara and her Phil delved into an engaging conversation. Seated at a cozy table, they shared laughter and thoughtful exchanges. He cut into a perfectly cooked steak, the juices glistening as he contemplated the complexities of relationships. "I'm too bad for a good girl like you," he mused, revealing a hint of self-awareness amidst.

Zara, with a playful spark in her eyes, responded with a touch of humor cloaked in sincerity. "Yeah, that would have been my answer too. But I had the Bible smart, book smart guy. Maybe I need all three." Her words hung in the air, blending wit with a genuine reflection on her past.

He contemplated her statement and replied, "Book smart, Bible smart, and what? Street smart," a grin slipping across his face as he looked at her. "And maybe I just need a good girl to balance my life out." The notion of balance resonated between them, a subtle recognition of their desire for stability amid the chaos of their experiences.

Taking a sip of her cool water, Zara shared, "I'm the only child too, " her voice soft yet steady. He nodded, his interest piqued, and then shared, "Same here," creating a rare bond over their shared upbringing. With a hint of admiration, he added, "Did I mention you look beautiful today?" He leaned back slightly, his eyes drinking in the sight of her. She wore a charming pink tank top that hugged her figure just right, and her gold earrings shimmered with every slight movement. Her lips, painted a delicate pink, appeared inviting and soft—almost as if they were meant for whispers and laughter. Her nails were a stylish medium length, impeccably manicured with pristine white tips that spoke of care and attention to detail.

Just as Zara opened her mouth to express her gratitude, her ex-boyfriend, Ester, approached with a commanding presence that immediately shifted the atmosphere. Tall and broad-shouldered, he stood at six feet, his long, wavy hair framing a handsome face that betrayed his underlying tension. His athletic build, honed from years on the football field, only amplified the jealousy that simmered beneath the surface as he laid eyes on Zara sharing a moment with another man.

"Zara," he called out, the intensity of his voice slicing through the easy camaraderie of their dinner. Zara's eyes narrowed slightly, her pulse quickening at the sight of him. "Ester, why are you here?" she replied, her irritation bubbling to the surface, ready to confront the unexpected intrusion. The air thickened with unspoken emotions, remnants of their past flickering like shadows, as the evening took a sudden and charged turn.

"I can ask you the same thing, Princess," he said, trying to lean down to kiss her on the cheek. Zara moves her face. "Don't!" She stands up, folding her arms across her chest. They've been done for months now. And she wasn't feeling him just walking up on her.

"Don't what?" He asked, getting upset. "You out going on dates I see," Ester football team comes in laughing and ready to eat.

"We've been done, Ester; it's no point in embarrassing yourself right now," Reminding him of the breakup. Ester gets close to Zara fast, making her step back, tripping over the chair leg, and falling in her seat. Phil gets up. "Is there a problem?" He asked, seeing Zara kinda scared of a skinny ass nigga like him.

"This ain't your problem," Ester eyes shifted towards Phil. Seeing him stand up stepping in front of Zara.

"It is now though, so what's sup?" Phil walks into Ester face.

"Yo, Phil. What's sup?" His cousin Rashawn comes up, shaking up with him. Rashawn was on the football team with Ester. He saw his cousin about to get mad. And he know his cousin have no temper what so ever. "Everything good," Rashawn asked, looking at Ester.

"Is it?" Phil asked, looking at Ester.

Zara was taken aback when she saw Phil confront Ester on her behalf. "Yo Ester, you don't want to do this with him," he said, standing his ground. Zara, still shaken, just wanted to leave. "Can we just go?" she asked, grabbing her purse and maneuvering around Ester as Phil regarded her intently. "Maybe next time," Ester retorted, to which Phil responded firmly, "It won't be a next time." Zara then took Phil's hand, and they walked away together.

As they strolled down the campus sidewalk ten minutes later, the night felt serene. The temperature was just right, with a gentle breeze brushing against Zara's face. Phil, dressed casually in cargo pants and a white tee, kept his hands in his pockets, embodying a simple yet appealing look. They passed by other students, some laughing, others dancing or reading, all enjoying the vibrant campus atmosphere.

Phil broke the silence by asking about Zara's ex-boyfriend. "So, ex-boyfriend?" he inquired. Zara let out a laugh, responding, "More like a fucking headache." When he pressed further, asking why they hadn't worked out, she explained, "He was too jealous, always wanted to be under me. Controlling. And the fights happened over the smallest things, like guys saying hi." Phil scoffed at the situation, surprised that her ex was still a student at their college. "All that, and he still get to stay all because he's the Dean son,"

"Damn. He ain't never put his hands on you did he?" He asked seeing Zara reject the question "You didn't have to say nothing, I can tell by the way he got up to you. Reason why I stepped up," he said as they walked into Zara building.

Zara walks up to the elevator doors clicking the button number to her floor. She turns around looking at Phil.

"Thank you for tonight. I've never enjoyed myself like I did today,"

"That means I get that number, right?" He asked handing over his phone smiling..

Zara laughs, taking his phone from his hands. She puts her number in, walking up to him kissing him on the cheek. The elevator doors opens. She step foot on the elevator turning around toward Phil waving goodbye as the door closed.

Chapter 11

Zara woke up at Jamie's house. The dream she just had, of how she met Phil in college always played over and over again. She felt like his presence is close by her. A tear drops from her face as she wipes it. Right now she was thinking on calling her dad. But then again, she couldn't. She got out of bed going into the kitchen seeing Jamie cooking breakfast.

"Hey," Zara said, seating down at the table.

"So, I've been thinking. Since you are scared to tell your dad. Why don't i?" Jamie said, bringing her a plate with bacon, eggs, hash browns, and side of sliced fruits. "Hear me out. Okay, I'll tell him you don't know that I know Killa killed Phil," She said

"Hell no," Zara's playful tone shifted as she warned Jamie about Killa's uncanny ability to read thoughts, as if he were diving deep their minds.

"Damn, you're right," Jamie replied, a hint of concern flickering in her eyes. "Well, what are we going to do?"

Zara shrugged, the uncertainty hanging in the air like a thick fog. Just then, her phone buzzed with a call from Killa, pulling her away from the moment. Her heart fluttered at the sight of his name, a mix of affection and worry swirling within her. Rising from her seat, she moved into the quiet of the extra bedroom Jamie had, seeking a moment away to chat.

"Hey, baby," she greeted, her voice veil of exhaustion betraying her otherwise cheerful demeanor.

"Are you okay?" Killa asked, his tone dropping to a concerned whisper as he sensed the lack of energy in her voice.

"Yeah, I just have a headache. I think I drank too much last night," she confessed, the memory of the previous evening dancing hazily in her mind.

"Still at Jamie's? I can swing by and bring you something for it," he offered, the warmth in his voice wrapping around her like a comforting blanket.

"I took a Tylenol, so hopefully it'll ease up soon. What do you have going on today?" Zara inquired, trying to shift the focus to him as her thoughts raced.

Killa exhaled slowly, taking a hit from his blunt. "I have a lot to move around today," he responded, the weight of responsibility evident in his voice. "But I really need to see you later."

Zara felt a small smile tug at her lips as she replied, "I'll text you."

He pulled the phone away from his ear to glance at the time, acknowledging the demands of the day ahead. "You ready?" His homebody asked. Killa shakes his head. Yeah, putting the phone back up to him ear. "Aye, I love you," he said, waiting for her to say something back. "Zara!"

"Ye—yes. Sorry, I love you too," she said, slapping her hand on her forehead.

"Talk to you later," Killa stood there for a minute, thinking why she was acting like that. She been weird since yesterday. He blew it off, walking upstairs out the basement.

"Alright, what we got?" Killa asked, coming up to the table seeing Dime and Nickle bags laying down ready. "Shit, this all you niggas made?" Killa asked getting upset.

"Yeah, we still got them hoes over there doing more," his homebody said.

"Nigga, we need to make ends meet, before shit goes left. This ain't gone cut it,"

"I got you. I'll have more within an hour," he responded.

"Nigga, all of it" Killa said walking out into the living room.

"Yo, Killa," a dude said, coming in. Killa turns around seeing Dee. Dee was around when Killa killed Phil. He came up just like them becoming Killa partner.

"Sup, D?" Killa shakes up with him

"Got a problem," Dee said, looking at him with a serious face.

"What is it?"

"Think that nigga Phil alive," he said seeing everybody stare at him.

"Nigga What?" Killa said knowing for sure he killed this nigga. "Tell me how you know?" Killa asked, crossing his arms across his chest.

"Swear, I've been seeing this nigga around. Driving in a black truck with tinted windows. Think it's a Lincoln. "

"You sure?" Killa asked

"I'm sure," Dee said, walking into the kitchen. Killa ain't believe it one bit. He know he killed that nigga. There is no way he is still living and ain't retaliate.

3 year earlier.

Zara and Phil leaving out the restaurant. Phil was captivated by Zara from the moment he first saw her in college. As he approached his BMW, he couldn't help but admire her style—ripped blue jeans, a fitted white top, and stunning white heels that showcased her toes. His heart raced as he took in her beauty before getting into the car.

Once inside, Phil affectionately rubbed her chin and remarked, "Baby, I won't lie; you had a lot of eyes on you today."

Meanwhile, Killa, driving a black truck with his friends, observed Phil's car from a distance. Curious about the stunning woman with him, he asked one of his friends if they knew who she was, but the response was a simple, admiring acknowledgment of her beauty. Killa instructed his friends to be careful, reminding them that they were only interested in Phil.

As Phil cruised down the highway at 60 mph, Killa followed a few cars behind, intrigued by Phil's destination. After half an hour, Phil exited into the suburbs, prompting Killa's friend to wonder who lived in that area. Killa shrugged, keeping a close watch on Phil's car.

Later that evening, at 8 PM, Phil turned to Zara and asked, "Did you enjoy yourself?" She smiled, grateful for the night they had spent together, feeling cherished and appreciated. "I did. Thak you for tonight baby," Zara said as they pulled up outside the house.

Phil got out of his car, shutting the door when a car pulled up, and a guy got out, coming around the car, seeing him reaching for the door handle. Killa points the gun at his head, shooting him. Zara screams, seeing Phil drop to the ground.

The car sped off, as Zara gets out running toward Phil side. Zara knelt on the cold, sterile floor beside her partner, her heart racing as she pressed her hands against his chest. Panic surged through her as she cried out, "No, no, no, please!" The desperation in her voice pierced the thick air as tears flooded her eyes. She felt the warmth of his breath faltering beneath her fingertips, and a chilling realization washed over her—he was barely holding on. "Baby, please," she implored, her voice choked with sorrow, her cries carrying the weight of her fear into the night. "SOMEBODY HELP ME!" Her voice rang like a siren, prompting concerned neighbors to rush out of nearby homes, drawn by the sound of her anguish.

Two hours later, Zara sat motionless in the waiting area, her body trembling. A napkin stained with dried blood lay crumpled in her hands, reminders of the chaos that had unfolded. She felt hollow, each attempt to speak only resulting in fresh waves of sobs escaping her lips. All she could wish for was that he would be okay; he was her heart, her everything. The room felt surreal as time warped around her; minutes dragged by like hours. Zara's mother and Phil's mother stood vigil at her side, their presence a quiet testament to shared grief. Yet, the weight of despair hung heavily in the air, mingled with the rhythmic beeping of monitors and the soft taps of nurses' slippers gliding past, each sound a reminder of the precarious balance between life and loss.

Suddenly, a male voice broke through the suffocating silence. "Mrs. Heathers," the doctor called, his demeanor somber as he approached.

Zara's heart raced as she looked up, desperate for good news. "Please tell me my son is okay?" she pleaded, her voice shaking with hope. But as the doctor lowered his gaze and then raised it again, his expression was grave. "I'm sorry for your loss," he said, each word a dagger to her heart.

In that moment, the world around Zara shattered. She fell to the floor, disbelief coursing through her as she struggled to comprehend the doctor's words. Phil's mother let out a heart-wrenching scream that echoed throughout the silent room, the sound of raw agony breaking the stillness and resonating in Zara's soul. The unbearable weight of grief enveloped them both, sealing their fates in a devastating reality they never wanted to face.

Chapter 12

3 years after his murder.

Phil wakes up in his hotel room. He was blessed to be alive. But he knows he couldn't be seen by anyone until the time was right. Zara was on his mind heavy as he looked out his window down at the water. It was cloudy, and it looked like it's about to rain. Phil stood there with his hands in his pocket, thinking.

"Phil," a man voice can be heard coming into his room..

Phil didn't bother to look back since who knew who it was. "Yes, Mark?" He asked, still looking down at the ocean..

"It's time," Mark said as Phil turned around, looking at him.

Phil grabs his coat from the couch, putting it on. He has been in Chicago for three years.

Phil stood at the precipice of his success, now a distinguished lawyer, but his mind was anchored in the past, swirling with memories of Zara. As he stepped out of his upscale hotel, the crisp air filled his lungs, and he slid behind the wheel of his sleek black truck, its engine purring to life. With purpose, he directed it toward the airport, each mile a reminder of the journey he had undertaken.

His phone buzzed, interrupting his thoughts. It was Mark, the bearer of news he had anticipated but dreaded. "Your mother has moved again," Mark said, his tone steady yet filled with unspoken weight. Phil felt a pang of concern; the constant upheaval in his mother's life often left him uneasy.

"And Zara?" he asked, a hint of tension lacing his voice.

"She's still with Killa," Mark replied, glancing up to meet Phil's gaze.

A flicker of anger ignited within Phil at the mention of Killa, but it quickly dimmed, replaced by a resigned understanding. He realized that Zara didn't truly know him, not the way he had known her. His thoughts drifted to that fateful night—had he crossed paths with her just before everything had changed?

As memories flooded back, Phil was transported six years into the past, where he found himself in the vibrant chaos of college life. He and Zara had spent months entwined in each other's worlds, their connection deepening with every walk back to her dorm. Each night, he would ensure she reached her door safely, cherishing the bond they were building.

One bright afternoon, he caught sight of her at a sign-up stand, the sunlight dancing in her hair. "Aye girl," he called out, sneaking up behind her with a playful grin. "Oh, so we signing up for dancing, huh?" His eyes sparkled with mischief.

Zara spun around, her arms instinctively wrapping around him in a warm embrace. "Been thinking about it," she said, a teasing smile lighting up her face. "Maybe I'll just be a boring ass cheerleader. You know," she added, stepping back to give him a twirl, showcasing her youthful spirit.

In that moment, time felt suspended, and the world around them faded away, leaving only the laughter and possibility of their shared future. Phil knew she was unlike anyone he had ever met, and in her presence, he felt both vulnerable and alive.

Phil laughs. "Hell nah, cheerleader ain't for your ass," he smiled. Zara walks back up to him, rubbing down his arms. She really liked Phil and wanted more as well. She was just afraid to ask him out.

"Zara!" Amber says, coming up, hanging her a bored. "Yeah, gone on head and joining the team back," Amber holds out the pen as Zara grabbed the board.

"Amber, who said I wanted to get back in?" Zara asked, smirking.

"Uhh. I see you signed your damn name for the dance team. Don't hold out on your girl. You know you was one of the best," Amber replies.

"Let me think about it," she sees Amber grab the board back, walking away.

Phil grabs Zara, turning her around. "So, why did you leave in the first place?" He asked, as the began to walk together.

"Drama. And I wasn't up for it. Jealousy as well," she said, making a weird face.

"Look at you. I'll be jealous too," Leaning in over kissing her neck.

"Stop. You know that tickles," grabbing his shirt. Phil got in her face, kissing her lips. "Let's go," he said, grabbing her hand and walking towards his car.

"Now you know we can't leave, right?" As they stopped in front of his car.

"They won't know we gone," he said, seeing Zara not move. "I'm playing. Come here, " he reached inside his car, grabbing out a small, long black jewelry box. Zara walks over to him, grabbing as he grabbed her hand while holding the box, and another hand.

"What you give me?" She asked smiling ear to ear.

"Something," Zara tries to reached for it. He pulls the box back. "Hold on now. First, tell me you'll be lady," he said, raising his eyebrows

"OH, so in order for me to get a gift, I'll have to say yes?" She asked, folding her arms across her chest. He shook his head yeah nervous for her answer.

Phil sat in silence, lost in the echoes of a cherished memory with Zara after five months of getting to know each other. He remembered the moment vividly: their playful banter, Zara teasingly interrupting him as he tried to express his feelings. "I just wanted to see what you'd do," she had said, a playful glint in her eye.

Phil had been earnest, revealing how she had become such an integral part of his life. "You've helped me with my work, spent countless hours by my side without judgment, even when my actions seemed off," he had confessed, grasping her hands gently at her waist.

His words were filled with sincerity as he tried to convey just how much Zara balanced him—she was everything he needed.

Zara, touched by his revelation, had felt tears welling in her eyes. "You're going to make me cry," she had said, her voice catching. The acknowledgment of their connection overwhelmed her as she admitted, "I've been happy ever since you came into my life." With a playful gesture, she held up two fingers and laughed, signaling her willingness to embrace their relationship fully: "So yes, I'd love to be that girl."

Phil had chuckled, shaking his head in mock disapproval. "Corny as hell," he had teased before leaning in to kiss her, sealing their bond with affection and laughter.

But as he returned to the present moment, the warmth of that memory contrasted sharply with the reality he faced. Tears streamed silently down his face as he sat there, lost in thought. He felt a profound ache in his heart, realizing just how deeply Zara had become his other half. The weight of his emotions was heavy, yet beneath the sorrow, a fierce determination stirred within him. Phil knew he had to fight to regain what they had lost.

With his hands pressed over his face, he rubbed his palms against his skin, hoping to quell the rising tide of pain. Taking a deep, steadying breath, he focused on the resolve to not only confront his emotions but to reclaim the love that had once brought him so much joy.

An hour later

"We'll be arriving in Atlanta, Georgia, here soon," a female pilot could be heard over the speakers.

Phil checks his phone. He knows he had guys back in the day who stayed in the game. But also stayed loyal to him. Either way, it goes, he was good on money.

Now that Zara's dad knows He's alive, he hopes he doesn't tell her before he does. All he wants is Killa behind bars.

Phil puts his phone down in front of him. He gets up from his private section on the plane going over to the bed. He was tired after dealing with a client back in Chicago under a different name. He takes his slippers off getting in the bed. He played back, closing his eyes.

Change 13

Week later.

Zara sits across from Killa while he eats what she cooks. He dug in his chicken, tearing it up with a side of Greens, Macaroni, and some cornbread. Zara East slowly started to lose all love for him. Phil was her other half. The man she planned on marrying and having kids by. Being with somebody who killed him will eat her alive slowly.

Killa leaned back in his chair, studying Zara across the table as she absentmindedly stirred her macaroni, a frown tugging at her lips. The air was thick with unspoken words, and he finally broke the silence. "Have you been quiet lately?" he asked, reaching for the napkin beside his plate to wipe his mouth clean.

Zara glanced up, her eyes shimmering with unshed tears, but she quickly masked her vulnerability. "No reason, baby," she replied softly, her voice barely above a whisper as she continued to poke at her food.

Killa's expression turned serious as he put the napkin down and took her hand gently in his own, urging her to meet his gaze. "Zara. Look at me," he said, his voice deep and steady. The weight of her feelings hung heavy between them. "What is it?"

"It's nothing, I've been feeling sick a lot lately," she admitted, forcing a smile to conceal the discomfort brewing inside her. Killa's brow furrowed, concern etched into his features. "You pregnant?" he asked bluntly, the implications of their recent choices hanging in the air.

Zara shook her head, trying to maintain her composure. "I've taken one. Says negative," she responded, her voice laced with uncertainty. He considered this, nodding slowly. "Probably wait another week. If so, would you keep it?" he probed, his tone a mixture of curiosity and apprehension.

Zara felt a flash of irritation. "Are you even ready to have kids? With everything you do?" The edge in her voice revealed the frustration she felt toward his carefree lifestyle. Killa sat up straighter, challenge sparking in his eyes. "What's that supposed to mean?"

"Baby, I'm not going to raise my child in the environment you create," she countered, her heart racing as the conversation escalated.

"If you are pregnant, you ain't got a choice," he said, his voice turning sharp, frustration bubbling to the surface.

"I have a choice. It's my body," Zara shot back, standing up with emotion flooding her voice as she invoked his real name, Rodrick. "The fuck is you saying?"

Killa's demeanor shifted, anger mixing with fear. "Zara, don't fucking play with my child. If you is pregnant…" His words trailed off, leaving a heavy silence filled with tension and uncertainty about their future.

Zara walks away from the table, while he just sits there continue eating. She hated arguing with him, cause he never shows he cares about her feelings. She slams her door getting in the bed. Good thing she wasn't pregnant, so she couldn't be that mad. Her phone rings seeing it's Jamie "Hey!" Zara answering aggressively

"Well damn, what I do?" She asked

"Nothing, had a little argument with Killa,"

"Girl, how are you holding up over there knowing what you know,"

"I'm good. Taking it day by day. You know me. I ain't going out like that," Zara said as Killa walked into the room, seeing her on the phone.

"Tell her you'll call her back," he said demanding.

"Why,?" Zara asked, coming up to her and hanging the phone up. "Okay, that was rude as fuck,"

"Zara, I know when something is up with you. So talk to me," he needed answers, and she wasn't just going ignore him all night why he left wondering.

"Babe, it's hard talking to you. You barely listen sometimes," she said

"I know I can be hard to deal with. Might not show emotion or show that I care. You know I love you to death. And would do anything for you," he paused seeing her tear up. "I ain't mean to act like that, I want a baby with you if you are pregnant. And if I move you away from this, I will," he comes up closer to her. He kissed her lips.

"I know. It's just hard sometimes for me too, babe," she said, "but I would love a baby with you. I never did say I didn't,"

Meanwhile (Phil arrived)

Phil hops in his black truck seeing his guys for the second time in months. He was happy they were good, and shit was always going straight. "Sup man, glad to see you back," his buddy Trell said

"A nigga always happy to be back home. How are things holding up?" He asked

"Nigga Killa getting low on product. Seeming like he needs some help. Zara has been keeping distance from him, though; she has been around Jamie a lot," Phil and Trell were seated in the truck, the heavy scent of rain-soaked asphalt filling the air as the rhythmic patter of raindrops drummed against the metal roof. The atmosphere was thick with tension, a shared understanding of the stakes weighing on their shoulders. Trell, leaning into the worn leather seat, broke the silence with a serious tone, "We need to keep a close watch on him. No matter what's going on, we can't drop our guard."

Phil nodded, his mind racing with thoughts as the windshield wipers swished back and forth, battling the relentless downpour. "Once we know where he's headed next, that's when we can make our move," he replied, his voice laced with determination.

"Just remember," Trell cautioned, his eyes narrowing slightly, "we've got everything under control as long as you stay clear of it. You know how unpredictable it can get."

Phil exhaled deeply, the momentary distraction of the rain fading as a wave of unease washed over him. "Good to hear," he managed, though the words felt heavy in his chest. "I just don't know how long this can go on. He's going to feel my presence soon enough." His thoughts spiraled, torn between a desire for justice and the darker impulse for revenge, the memory of the previous attempt on his life burning in his mind.

As the truck rolled to a stop in front of his mother's house, a flash of nostalgia swept through him, mingled with apprehension. The familiar sight of the modest, weathered home brought back a flood of memories. It had been far too long since he had seen her — far too long since he had felt the warmth of her love. This visit was more than a mere reunion; it was a chance to reclaim a part of himself that had been missing since his father had disappeared into the shadows of their past.

Gathering his thoughts, Phil stepped out of the truck, the chill of the rain-soaked air nipping at his skin as he approached the front door. With each step, anticipation danced in his chest. When his mother finally opened the door, the look on her face was a mixture of bewilderment and profound joy.

She stood there, her eyes widening as tears welled up, glistening like pearls against her weathered skin. For a moment, time stood still; the world around them faded as her emotions surged, unfiltered and pure. She raised a trembling hand to cover her mouth, stifling a gasp of disbelief.

Unable to fully process the reality of his presence, she reached out instinctively, her fingers grazing his chest as if to assure herself that he was truly there. The moment their skin connected, an electric surge of recognition spread through both of them, filling the air with an unspoken bond. The warmth of her touch wrapped around him like a comforting blanket, a reminder that he was home again, standing before the woman who had always been his guiding star amid a turbulent life.

Phil caught her, picking her up taking her inside the house. Things still look the same, with some new furniture. He lays her down on the couch as Trell comes in with a wet rag putting over her head. He rubs her face shedding a tear.

An hour later

Ms. Rose woke up touching Phil again, shocked. "Baby, tell me this a dream," she said, touching him with both her hands.

He cries, shaking be head no. She grabs his face, wiping his tears. She hugged him so tight and never wanted to let. "Where have you've been?" She asked

"Had to find out who killed me, ma. I couldn't just show my face right away," he said, seeing his mother look into his eyes.

"You're never leaving my side," as tears came storming down her face too.

Phil smiles, knowing his mother is serious. "I never left, ma. I love you," he said, kissing her forehead.

"Who was it, baby?"

Phil shakes his head, knowing his mother is going to be mad. Killa was like a second son to her. She practically raised him herself when his mother didn't have much.

"Just know it was someone close to me. I just don't need you telling anybody I'm back. You hear me, ma, nobody can't know," he said

"You know momma will always have your back," she said, kissing his forehead over and over.

Chapter 14

8 pm

Dennis and his wife. Made dinner tonight, inviting their daughter and Jamie. Źara walks in, smiling, talking to Jamie.

"Mom, Dad," Zara said, taking off her coat. She walked through the living room towards the kitchen. The table was adorned with a delightful array of dishes, the aroma of freshly cooked food wafting through the air and beckoning Jamie to take a seat. Without hesitation, she settled down and flashed a satisfied smile at the spread before her. Debra glided over, her hands cradling elegant glasses of wine that she placed before Jamie and the other girls, her warmth enveloping them like a comfortable blanket.

"How are my babies doing?" Debra asked, her eyes sparkling with affection as she took a seat among them. Jamie, brimming with excitement, replied, "The shop's been going great! Sales have been through the roof." Just as she poised her fork to dive into her meal, Dennis piped up, a playful grin on his face, reminding her, "Now, Jamie, you say grace."

"Dammit," she muttered under her breath with a mock exasperation. With a touch of dramatics, she gathered everyone's hands and grinned, "Okay-Okay. Hands together, ladies and gentlemen." Zara chuckled at Jamie's antics, clearly enjoying the moment. With a cheerful tone, Jamie pronounced, "God is good, God is great. Thank you for our food. Thank you for everything you blessed us with. Amen." Zara looked at her with an amused expression, prompting Jamie to tease, "What?"

"OH nothing. Amen," Zara replied with a grin, picking up her fork and eagerly diving into her rich, cheesy lasagna.

As the meal continued, Dennis turned his attention to Zara and asked, "How are you and what's-his-name Shawn doing?" He wiped his mouth with a napkin, his demeanor shifting to one of concern. Zara paused, her enthusiasm waning. "We're okay," she admitted slowly, her voice tinged with uncertainty. "I just don't know if I still want this relationship. I still think about Phil." A shadow seemed to pass over her face, and she fell silent, the weight of her thoughts making her momentarily introspective and wishful. Zara wanted to tell her parents what she knows. And her dad asking the question right off back gone have her spill it out. Phil has always been a touchy subject to her now.

"Babygirl, it's okay to talk about it," Dennis said

"Every time I sleep now. I think about how we met, him being shot," With tears coming down her face. "I'm not over him being gone. I'm not ready to give my all into Shawn knowing he fucking killed him—

She just blurted out. At this point she ain't care, cause why would he do that to him. What was the reason?

"WHAT?" Debra said looking at her confused.

Zara cries even harder. "Ma, he killed Phil. And I was scared that if he finds out I know something about it, he might do the same. I love that man to death, too. I just—

Dennis gets up, hugging his daughter in a warm embrace, his voice steady and reassuring as he declared, "Think I'm going to let anything happen to you? I'm your father, your protector. I'll always have eyes on you. You hear me?" He pressed a gentle kiss on her forehead, a gesture filled with love and promise.

Curiosity flickered in Debra's eyes as she turned to Jamie, asking, "How did you find out?"

Jamie took a breath, recalling the earlier moment. "She overheard him on the phone after she told him hours before about what happened to Phil. Killa never knew Zara dated Phil."

Debra's eyebrows knitted together in surprise as she pressed further, "And you didn't know either?" Her gaze fixed on Jamie, knowing she had been part of that world.

"Well, no. Of course, I wouldn't know Killa killed Phil," Jamie replied, a hint of defensiveness creeping into her tone.

Debra softened her approach, sensing Jamie's tension. "I wasn't saying that, baby," she reassured. "Yes, you went to school together, but they haven't spoken in over a decade—at least, that's what I thought." Jamie's honesty shone through her voice as she elaborated, "I never even thought to bring up the relationship between Phil and Killa; we were just kids back then."

Debra pulled Jamie into a comforting hug, whispering, "I wasn't accusing you of anything. I just wanted to know." Stepping back, she made a decision to ease the tension in the room. "Look, you girls should stay here tonight. Your rooms are just as you left them."

A moment later, Zara approached, her face lighting up as she kissed her mother softly on the cheek before heading upstairs, her footsteps echoing softly on the stairs as she disappeared from view, leaving the warmth of the moment lingering in the air. Once Debra hears the door shuts. She turns towards Dennis. "So?" She asked waiting for him to do something.

"I see why Phil kept his identity a secret. Killa was his bestfriend and close to him. I'll be back," he said, grabbing his keys and jacket, walking out the door

(Phil Hotel)

Dennis walks in Phil Hotel and sees him standing there. Phil stood frozen, a swirl of anxiety gripping his chest as Dennis's words sank in. "Shawn?" he murmured, disbelief etched across his face. The room felt stifling, the air thick with tension. Dennis continued, casually wiping his mouth and shoving his hands deep into his pockets. "Zara just told me she overheard him talking about killing you."

A wave of pain washed over Phil, and he couldn't help but feel the sharp sting of betrayal. "She must have told him about me," he replied, his voice heavy with realization, the hurt evident in his tone. The thought that Zara might care for Rodrick enough to disclose his secret life twisted his insides. "I need to see her," he added, the urgency in his voice only amplifying his turmoil.

Dennis, however, was quick to interject. "Think that's a good idea?" he asked, a cautious glance in his direction.

Phil began pacing, each step fueled by the desperation swirling inside him. "She needs to know I'm alive. I can't wait another year for her to find out I'm dead when I'm not," he insisted, the words tumbling from him with a mix of frustration and fear.

"You can't show your face," Dennis countered, his voice firm. "She will not want to be around him. It's safer for her to believe you're gone." He watched as Phil marched back and forth, clearly torn between his love for Zara and the reality of their precarious situation.

Dennis knew Phil's heart—he was a devoted father who would never raise a hand against her nor argue with her when emotions ran high. Patience was his virtue; he always waited for her anger to cool before gently encouraging her to find a solution together.

Stepping closer, Dennis placed a comforting hand on Phil's shoulder, grounding him. "I know this must be incredibly hard for you. But you have to keep doing what you're doing. You're smart, Phil; I'll give you that." He took a deep breath, knowing the weight of the moment. "I have to be back to work tomorrow, but just remember," he added softly, "Zara's safety has to come first. You know I will not be able to leave, make sure she has extra eyes on her. Please, not until I get back Phil," Dennis said, stepping in front of him.

"I'll try my best," he said, seeing Dennis walk around him and out his hotel room.

Phil didn't know if he should do something now or wait. He just knew he wasn't going to waste another year not holding his baby.

Change 15

3 days later.

Killa was home going through his security cameras. He always checked inside and out, just to be safe. Making sure, nobody watching or sitting outside his crib. He hasn't spoken to Zara since yesterday morning. He doesn't know what's been up with her. Looking over from inside the house, he goes to the night where he was on the phone with Dee conversation about Killa. He saw Zara come out sneaking up hearing the conversation. He gets up now, knowing why she was acting like that. He grabs his phone calling her.

Zara stirred awake in the familiar surroundings of her childhood bedroom, sunlight filtering through the curtains and illuminating the dust motes dancing in the air. She had sought refuge at her parents' house for the past few days, needing time to recover from the emotional turmoil that resulted from confiding in them about what she had overheard from Killa.

Rubbing the sleep from her eyes, she noticed her phone buzzing incessantly on the charger, its screen lighting up with Killa's name more times than she could count. Concerned, she quickly swiped to call him back, her heart racing a little as she did. "Hey baby. Are you okay?" she asked, her voice laced with worry as he answered.

"Where you at?" Killa's voice came through, thick with longing.

"I've been at my parents'. I had to spend some time with my dad before he leaves for work," she replied, swinging her legs over the side of the bed and feeling the cool floor beneath her feet.

"I need to see you. I miss you. Let me come pick you up," he said, a sense of urgency in his tone as he drove through the city streets.

"Okay. Just give me a bit to get dressed and grab something to eat. I'll call you in about an hour," Zara assured him, her heart fluttering at the thought of seeing him.

After they hung up, Zara padded down the narrow hallway and descended the staircase, the wooden steps creaking softly under her weight. When she reached the living room, she was momentarily surprised to find her brother Jamie sprawled on the couch, his eyes glued to the screen as the news flickered in front of him.

"Since when did you watch the news?" she teased playfully, glancing at him as she made her way into the kitchen.

"Never," he shrugged, getting up to follow her. "So, I heard you on the phone. Was it Killa?"

Their exchange filled the air with an undercurrent of sibling concern, as Zara prepared to meet Killa, her heart weighing heavy with unspoken emotions. "Yeah. He gone come pick me up in an hour," she said, grabbing a bowl out of the cabinet.

"I don't think you should go," Jamie said, starting to feel concerned about her.

"I ain't seen him a three days. And we have barely been talking now. I already look suspicious. Or like something off, I can't have that," she said, pouring her some frosted flakes.

"Im coming with you then," Jamie took Zara bowl of cereal eating it.

Zara and Jamie were enjoying a playful moment in the kitchen, laughter bubbling between them like the frothy milk in the bowl. Jamie, still chuckling, misinterpreted Zara's intentions, thinking she had prepared the bowl just for her. Milk dribbled from the corner of her mouth as she stifled her giggles. Zara, with a warm smile, playfully waved the misunderstanding away and reached for another bowl. "Anyways, I think I'll be okay. You have my location," she said with a hint of reassurance in her voice.

Jamie's expression shifted slightly as her concern resurfaced. "I just want you to be safe. Killa is dangerous," she warned, her eyes reflecting genuine worry. Zara, however, brushed off the concern with a lightheartedness that belied the gravity of the situation. "I know he is," she replied with a twinkle of mischief. "But he claims he loves me. I guess if he ever found out what I really thought, hopefully, he wouldn't kill me," she added with a giggle, as if the thought were a mere joke. There was a flicker of carefree confidence in her demeanor, suggesting she didn't truly believe Killa would harm her.

Hours later, Zara sat comfortably on the plush couch in Killa's living room, the soft glow of ambient lighting creating an intimate atmosphere. Killa moved about the room, the sound of glass clinking as he retrieved a bottle of wine from the kitchen. He reentered the room, a warm smile playing on his lips as he poured a rich red into two glasses. The room felt charged with anticipation as he settled next to Zara, watching her take a slow sip, savoring the flavor.

"How are your parents?" he asked, leaning back and studying her.

"They are fine. Still going strong," she answered, her gaze flickering to him as he edged closer, a subtle intimacy washing over them.

"And you? It's been three days since I've seen you," Killa remarked, his voice gentle but firm.

Zara sighed, attempting to convey her reasoning. "I've told you why, though," she replied, her tone light yet contemplative.

"Zara, I've been with you for a minute now. You still could manage to see me for at least a few hours when you go out," Killa said, his concern mingled with a hint of longing, as if he were pleading for reassurance of their bond amidst the complexities of their lives. "Stop playing with me,"

"I'm not playing with you, Shawn. I just –" she paused, seeing him stare right into her eyes.

She knows when Killa thinks something off or is about to be upset. He sits his drink down, grabbing her face. "What all you hear?" He asked

"What?" She said while he held her face.

"Zara, I love you. But tell me, what did you hear that night I was on the phone?" He asked, seeing her get afraid.

Zara begins to cry. Killa let go of her cheeks. He stood up, knowing she heard everything.

"You told Jamie, didn't you?" He asked, looking down at her crying. He grabs her hand, making her stand up. He loved her. But now his mind thinking otherwise. "I know you. The club. You staying all night with her all of a sudden," he said, grabbing her neck, making her look up at him.

Zara grabs his arm, feeling him squeeze her a little tighter. "Shaw—" she tried saying his name but she couldn't due to him squeezing her neck harder and harder.

Killa, let's go, not wanting to do that to Zara. She was his heart and maybe pregnant with his baby. Zara grabs her neck, rubbing down her shoulder, with her hand. She felt that. At this point, she was scared for her life.

Killa tries to grab her hand, but she yanks from him running towards the door. Killa ran after her, grabbing her from behind.

"Where you going?" He said, throwing her on the ground. He shakes his head, not wanting to hurt her at all. He pulled out his phone, calling Dee.

"Yeah, come meet me at my house," Killa said, hanging up. He walks back up to Zara, who is scooting back on the floor. He grabs her legs, pulling her towards him.

"Shawn, get off me. Just let me go," she said, seeing his grab her arms.

"I can't let you leave," He picked her up. He carries her to the room, throwing her down on the bed.

"I'm not going to say anything," With tears coming down her face.

He grabs her arm, pinning it up to the bed frame tying her hands to them. Then he did the same with her feet. He climbs on top of her, whipping her face.

"You know I love you, right?" He said

"If you love me. Why tie me up?" She asked, sobbing to him. "Why do this? When you could have told me you killed Phil, you could have told me," she said

"I couldn't," he said, kissing her forehead and climbing off her. He walks out of his bedroom, shutting the door.

Chapter 16

Killa waited until Zara was sleeping to move her. He had slipped her a sleeping pill in her juice while she was tied up to the bed. He walks in, seeing her head tilt over.

12 am

He unties her, moving her hair from her face. He kisses her cheek, picking her up. He walks out of his bedroom with Zara on his shoulders.

"Ready?" Dee asked, seeing him come out with Zara. Dee opens the backdoor and walks out.

Killa puts Zara in the back, buckling her up. He went around the other side to sit in the back with her, just in case she woke up.

Dee pulls off.

(Reminiscing)

"Baby!" Zara said, coming from out of her bedroom with this all-gray dress on that was a little past her knee. She walks in front of Phil, showing off her dress. "And how you like?" She asked, turning around for him.

Phil gets up seeing her smile. "Baby, you always look good with whatever you put on," he grabbed her waist.

"And so does my man," she said, wrapping her arms around his neck.

Phil picks her up, putting her on the dresser. Passionately kissing Zara, he unzipped her dress, taking it off slowly.

Zara feels his soft hands rub down her back, which makes her body tingle. His touch always made her horny. There was always something about Phil that Zara always gave in to when it came down to him touching her body.

Phil scooted Zara to the edge, undoing his belt while still kissing her. He drops his pants, taking his dick out through his boxers. He sticks it inside Zara, hearing her moan. He picks her back up, making her come down on dick.

"I love you, baby," Zara moaned as he looked up, kissing her.

"I love you too," he said, putting her back down on the dresser as he sped up the pace, kissing her neck.

(Killa's other house)

Zara sits down in a chair with just her hands tied together. Killa sits in front of her not saying anything.

"So what you thinking?" Dee asked, coming down the steps.

"I don't know yet," He said, getting up while Zara watched him walk away.

"Just get over with," Zara was tired of just sitting there being around him. She knew he wouldn't kill her. She just wanted to see what he'll do.

"I ain't gone kill you, Zara," he said, lighting his blunt.

Zara phone starts ringing. Over and over again. Killa picks it up seeing it, Jamie calling. Than her mother. He turns her phone completely off.

"That ain't gone do nothing but make them suspicious,"

"Baby, let them think what they want. I ain't scared of nobody. You know that,"

"Why did you kill him?" Zara asked, wanting to know..

Killa walks back over to her with his blunt in his hand. He sits down.

"I don't know," He honestly said. Phil was his partner and best friend. He really didn't have a reason to kill him. He was fucked up about it for a while. And regretted it.

"You don't know? WHAT TYPE OF FUCKING ANSWER IS THAT? HE WAS EVERYTHING TO ME," Zara yells. She was furious to hear that. You killed him for no reason was not the answer she was looking for. "You killed him for no reason," Zara said, putting her tied hands on her face crying. "He was your best friend,"

"You still love him, I see," he said, standing up, feeling some type of way.

Zara, shakes her head. "After I've told you he got killed. Why didn't you just say something?" She asked, whipping her face.

"Tell his girl I was the one who murdered him. You sound dumb as fuck. I ain't know you was even his girl," he said

"But you knew after and still led me on to thinking you never done anything to him. Knowing he was your best friend. Fuck!" She said, hitting her hands repeatedly on her thighs. She was so hurt. She fell in love with Phil's best friend.

"Because we already had built something. My feelings and all that shit were in the way. And I'm in love with yo ass. So yeah, I kept it a secret and you around. I didn't give a fuck at that point,"

"Didn't give a fuck about what? Me? Or him?"

"Him. I couldn't let you go that easy, baby. And I'm still not," he was serious about not hurting Zara. That was his baby.

"So, keep me hidden. Locked up, tied up?" She asked

"Yeah, that's what I'm thinking. I can't see myself hurting you. And I still don't even know if you're pregnant," he said

Zara shakes her head again.

Chapter 17

Debra and Jamie have been blowing up Zara phone for hours now. Debra informed her husband that she felt like something bad happened to her. Debra received a knock at the door. Her and Jamie look at each other.

"I'll go answer it," Jamie said, getting up.

Jamie gets up, walking to the door. She looks through the peep hole seeing Phil. She pushed her head back, confused. Then, looked again. This time, she swings open the door Debra stood in shock, her eyes wide as she confronted Phil, who had unexpectedly returned from the dead. Overcome with emotion, she rushed to him, tears streaming down her face as she embraced him tightly. "I'm so glad you finally showed up," she exclaimed, relief flooding her voice.

Just then, Jamie re-entered the living room, confusion etched on her face. "Wait. So you knew he was alive?" she asked, scratching her head. Debra simply nodded, and Jamie's thoughts turned to Zara, who had been missing for hours. "Zara's going to trip out," Jamie muttered under her breath.

"She's been with him?" Phil asked, anger rising within him as he realized he'd lost track of Zara's whereabouts. Jamie confirmed, "I told her not to go, but you know how she is."

Determined, Phil prepared to leave. "Well, I have to bring back the old me," he said, ready to take action. Jamie, sensing his intensity, stopped him and wrapped him in a heartfelt hug, embracing the moment of reunion and the uncertainty that lay ahead. Now her best friend ain't got anything to be sorry about.

"I'm glad you back, bro," Jamie said

"Me too, sis," He hugged her back, than walked out the door. Phil gets in his car.

"What we about to do?" Trell asked, sitting there hitting his blunt.

"He still got that spot on the north side?" Phil asked

"You know that's where all his stash is. Let roll through," he said

Phil sits back as they drove off. Him and Killa bought that house when they made they first hundred thousand dollars together. He was stupid to still have that place.

"How are you feeling?" Trell asked.

"Angry," Phil said. He had a plan out for Killa. Instead of killing him. He wants to talk first. He wants to see where his head is. Did he care about killing me? Did he even think before he did that shit? Phil needed answers before he did something stupid next.

3 am

Killa already moved spots. He ain't have a good feeling about the house him and Phil bought together. He knows Zara father probably got somebody looking for her already. Killa looks over at Zara sound asleep. He felt bad for doing this to her. But he got to look out for himself too.

They headed on highway getting out of Georgia. Took them an hour or two to get to where they was going. As they drove through the unfamiliar terrain, Zara stirred awake, her heart racing. The vehicle had come to a stop in front of a house she didn't recognize. Confusion washed over her as she asked, "Where are we?" Her hands were still bound, a harsh reminder of her situation.

"Just stay cool," Killa replied calmly, pulling out a knife to free her wrists. Zara quickly rubbed her sore skin, noticing a mark from the rope. Killa then stepped out and opened her door, extending his hand to her. "Baby, come on," he urged, and she hesitantly took his hand, allowing him to help her out.

Approaching the door, Killa knocked patiently. Moments later, a bearded man—tall and resembling Killa—answered. "Sup bro?" he greeted, exchanging a fist bump. His eyes flicked to Zara with curiosity. "What you doing here? And who's she?"

"This is my lady. We need a place to stay for a while," Killa said, brushing past him into the living room. The man's expression shifted, probing further. "Yo, what you do this time?" he inquired, shutting the door behind them.

"Nothing," Killa deflected, not wanting to reveal the truth. "I just need to keep my lady safe for now." As he spoke, a tension lingered in the air, signaling that though they were inside, their troubles were far from over..

"Sup, I'm Cameron," he said holding out his hand.

Zara didn't shake it. "Zara," she said looking afraid at first. She let it brush off though.

"This my brother. Same daddy, different mother," Killa said

"And you never told me," she said folding her arms across her chest. "And I'm tired,"

"Come on," Killa said as she got up. He grabs her hand going up the steps. Killa walks down to the end of the hall opening up the last door.

Zara walks in behind him looking around. She walks into his room, seeing Killa's name on the wall and some pictures of him and Phil as a kid. Zara shakes her head not wanting to even sleep in here. Looking at Phil and then at Killa. She just started to hate herself for it. But she wasn't going be in this relationship if she ain't dead yet.

"I'm sorry," He said seeing her grab a picture of him and Phil.

Zara just couldn't stop shaking her head "You not sorry. How can you have a of you two, and you did that to him?" She asked

"Never came back here. Honestly, I forgot those were even up there. I ain't bring you in here to make you cry. You already think I want to hurt you, and I don't," he said, coming up to her.

"For a person who almost choked me to death," she said seeing him grab her face.

She instantly puts her hands on top of his just holdfing them.

"I ain't mean to do that," he said looking at her in the eyes. "Ain't lie when I said I loved you. I just can't have you running to your pops, telling them what you know. Which Jamie probably said something already,"

"I—I just don't know what to say anymore," she said, seeing him grab her hand, holding them.

"Tell me you love me," he said close to her face.

"You know I love you. If I can be real. This is all so much. I can't be myself right now. I can't show you that side of love right now. When I overheard you talk about him, like you ain't care. You look at me as a trophy," she said, tears still running down her face. "If I wanted my parents to know, they would have done something. They didn't. So you didn't have to do this," she said, whipping her face and letting go of his hands.

"I didn't see that at first, but I fell in love with you, Zara. You special, and I can't lose you,"

"And I didn't want to lose you," she said, turning her back on him. She was hurt as fuck.

All these emotions run through Zara's head. She just wanted to run away from it all herself. Her favorite person is gone. She fell in love with his best friend who killed him. Now she kidnapped? Yeah, she was over it.

Chapter 18

Phil pulls up in the back of Him and Killa old house. It still looks the same. Modern, white on the outside. The grass didn't look like it was cut for months. And Phil hated that. He noticed there weren't any cars there, and there were no lights on.

Phil gets out, walking towards the back door with his gun out. He grabbed his keys out, that he still had from when he left. He tried to unlock it, and it worked.

Trell moved him out way, going in first. The house was a mess from the back to the front. Phil went straight to the basement. He sees a chair with rope around it. He see weed spread out like nobody knew how to clean up after themselves.

"Take all his shit," Phil said as Trell and a few other of his boys came down, grabbing the drugs and pills.

Phil gets to thinking about everybody him and Killa grew up around him. And it wasn't to many niggas to think about since they only trusted a few.

"Let's ride to Alabama," Phil said, grabbing his phone out and seeing Dennis (Zara Father). Calling. "Yes, sir," He said

"Give me something. Do I have to come?" He asked.

"Everything is fine. I'll let you know what else I find," he said, hanging up.

Phil leaves out the house, locking up. And when Killa decides to come back, he'll know exactly who's been in here. Only him and Phil had a key. Phil hops in his car driving off hitting the highway.

(Next morning)

Killa left Zara back in Alabama while he comes back to Georgia. He still had work to do and get that shit cleaned up from his crib on the north.

"You good?" Dee asked

"Got a funny ass feeling bro," he looks out the window .

They pulled back up to his crib getting out. They walked in the front door seeing shit still in the same place. Killa walks down to the basement seeing his product gone..

"What the fuck?" He said standing there putting his hands in his pockets.

Dee comes down the step seeing the table cleared and the shelf where the cocaine was gone.

"Bro, don't tell me somebody took our shit," Dee couldn't come to the fact somebody had come and taken their shit, and nobody had a key besides Killa. They just re-up. Now they have to do this shit all over again. More money was lost this time. Killa raised his eyebrows turning towards Dee.

"You said you've seen Phil?" Killa remembered him saying that just the other day.

"Yeah, but nigga been high as fuck lately. Why?" Dee asked.

"I think he's alive," Killa said

"Nigga you shot him in the head. Ain't no way the nigga lived," he said

"Who else had a key to get in? Nothing was touched upstairs nor ran through. Not even the backdoor was broken into. Think nigga. He was the only one who had the key to this house. Nigga our house, " he said

Killa took off upstairs. He ran out the door, grabbing his phone. He starts dialing his brother's number.

(Killa brother house)

Phil and his guys get out of the car walking up, knocking on the door. Cameron walks to the door. As he opened it. Phil stood before him.

"Phil?" He said, seeing him standing in his all-black suit, dreads freshly done.

Phil homeboys rushed him, stealing off Cameron.

"Tie that nigga down," Phil said seeing if he's the only one in here. Phil pulls out his gun walking towards the kitchen. He puts his back on the wall peeping around seeing nobody.

He walks back into the living room, seeing Cameron getting tied up to the chair. Phil begins to walk up the steps slowly.

He comes to the top of the steps, putting the silencer on his gun. He walks to every bedroom, opening them slowly pointing his gun.

He gets to the last bedroom at the end. Which he knew was Killas room. He slowly opens the door, seeing a body laying under the cover. He points to the gun coming in. Long, pretty curly hair was seen as he got closer.

Phil pulls the cover back a little, seeing its Zara sound asleep. He took a deep breath, trying not to shed a tear. He puts his gun up in his front pants sitting down in front of her and just watch her breath slowly. Her skin was still golden. Her hair grew longer, her lips was soft and pink.

Zara moves thinking its Killa. "Killa, move. Please," she moved her hair out her face. When she looks up, she pops up so fast, scooting back on the bed in shock.

Zara hearts starts racing. Her hands went over her mouth as she thinks it's dream. Tears filled up her eyes seeing Phil touch her. Zara sits with her legs in a criss cross position as her head fell into her hands. She couldn't believe what she was seeing.

"Come here baby," Phil said with tears coming down his face. He grabs Zara hand feeling it shake.

Zara gets up wrapping her arms around him digging her face in his chest. And she wasn't letting go.

Phil was crying just as hard. "I love you, I love you," he all he kept saying.

"Tell me this ain't me dreaming Phil?" She asked while her face still dug into his chest.

"No, it ain't," he squeezed her tight.

"I'm so sorry," she said, sobbing. She began to stomp her leg in hurt knowing she was dating somebody Who she thought killed him.

"Ain't your fault," he said. He grabs her shoulder, making her look up at him. "What's sup baby?" He asked, smiling with tears in his eyes.

"What's sup, baby?" Zara said giggles with tears running down her face, as she rubs his cheeks. "I love you so much," she said

"I love you," He was still holding her waist, looking into her eyes. "Just beautiful, always been,"

Coming back to reality, Zara hits him.

"Why you ain't tell me you was alive?" She asked folding her arms.

"Couldn't," he said. "But we have other days to talk about that. Right now, I just want to look at you," he said, grabbing her face and kissing her, rubbing her tears off.

Zara passionately kissed him back. She closed her eyes, feeling his lip touch her. "Soft," he whispers. Zara smiles. She opens her eyes seeing him look down at her.

"Let's go," he grabbed her hand, walking towards the door.

She stops. "Where's Killa?"

"Probably back at our house in Georgia. And trust me. He knows I'm back by now, "

Chapter 19

Walking out Killa room holding Zara hand, they walked downstairs seeing Cameron still tied up. "You good?" Trell asked, standing there.

"Yea," Phil said, letting go of Zara hand. He walks over to Cameron, taking the tape of his mouth.

"What the fuck is this?" Cameron asked with blood dripping on his shirt, from his lips.

"Trying to figure that out myself. Where is your brother?" Phil asked, leaning down and looking at him.

"You know,"

Phil's laughter filled the air as he approached Cameron, who was sitting alone, lost in thought. "What's up, man? How have you been?" He flashed a casual grin while pulling a chair in front of him and settling down, trying to break through the heaviness of the moment.

Cameron's expression darkened slightly as he replied, "I've been handling my own shit, you know? That is until Shawn ass showed up. Phil turns around moving seats, sitting down. "We gone wait until the nigga come," he said grabbing his phone out telling Zara dad she was good.

Zara sees more of Phil homeboys come in never seeing them before.

"Sup?" One of them said shaking up with Phil. "What we got?" He asked looking over at Cameron than Zara.

"We gone wait for the nigga to come," Phil reminds him

His homeboy giggles "he fucked up now huh? Brung my nigga old side out," Hearing a car pull up. Phil gets up already knowing it's him. "Baby get over here behind me," he said grabbing his gun out. And all his homeboys did too.

Killa runs in with his gun drawn with Dee. Stood around him was 8 niggas. And Phil stood right in front of him.

"Sup?" Phil said, holding his gun in his hand.

"Zara—

"Don't even speak her name, bruh. What's sup? You see me," Phil stood firm waiting for this nigga to speak. And he better speak likely.

Killa didn't know what to say, honestly "I do. What's sup?" He looks over at Zara, who looks scared.

"You tell me? A nigga who taught you everything, a nigga who grew up starting this shit. Buying that house you still selling out of. Nigga I made you who you are," Phil said wanted to yell but he kept it coo.

"Man—

"Man WHAT? SPEAK NIGGA. CAUSE MY PATIENT RUNNING OUT," Phil becameangry yellimg. Because this nigga ain't have no reason, doing the shit he did.

"You THINK I WANTED TO DO THAT SHIT?"

"NIGGA YOU DID. AINT DO SHIT BUT CHOSE A BETTER LIFE. WAS YOU JEALOUS? I ASKED YOU TO COME WITH ME. I TOLD YOU AS YOUR BESTFRIEND, ILL ALWAYS HAVE YOU NIGGA," Phil continues to yell

"I'm sorry bro. A nigga sorry man," Killa puts his hand on top of his head.

Phil was so heated.

"Okay, you sorry?" Phil asked, looking at him crazy

"What do you want? You got my brother tied up,"

"Nigga I don't give a fuck. You gone feel me," Phil said turning around stealing off his brother.

Killa tries to step forward, but Trell stops him. Killa watched as Phil repeatedly steal off on him seeing more blood come out his mouth..

"Come on Phil!" Killa said

Zara stood there in shock, never seeing this side of him. But she understood and let him do what he needed to do. Phil turns around pointing his gun at Killa knee letting off a silent shot. Killa falls to the ground grabbing his knee.

"FUCK!" He said

Phil walks up to him pointing the gun at his head. Zara walks over grabbing his arm. She looks up at him breathing heavy, and not thinking at that point. She needed to step in. Zara rubs his face making him look down at her. He shed a tear pointing the gun down.

"Balance right?" He asked staring at Zara.

"Yes—yes. Balance baby," she said as he tucked the gun back in front of his pants, walking back to sit down. Zara turns around, looking at Killa.

"Zara,"

"Umhum," With tears coming down her face. She felt bad, and she didn't want to see him dead.

"I'm sorry for everything. Im dead ass. Look at me, man," he sits up on his ass with blood gushing out his knee. Zara looks at him as she folds her arms across her chest.

"I ain't mean to scare you. I just want you to know I should have listened to you more,"

Phil sits back hearing Killa pour his heart out to Zara, just listening. He wasn't hurt by what he was saying. He knew Zara was a good girl. She never cheated, and always stayed in her bag. She just wanted to be babied here and there. And it seemed like Killa wasn't giving that, which he knew.

"I don't even know if you're pregnant, " he said

Zara turns her head slightly, looking over her shoulder at Phil sitting up. She looks back at Killa. "I'm not pregnant, Killa,"

"How you know?"

"I was faking. I had to play like nothing was wrong when I found out you've killed Phil," she said. "Then you said, you wouldn't know what to do with me if I did find out. You choked me, " she said with more tears forming.

"He choked you?" Phil asked, getting up about to walk up to Killa, but Zara stopped him.

"He eventually stopped. But it scared the fuck out of me," she said

"Zara, I'm sorry. Can I get a towel or something? I'm just bleeding out,"

Zara looks around at nobody moving. She rolls her eyes, going to get a towel and coming back, giving it to him.

Dennis walks in with his bodyguards seeing Killa on the floor and Phil standing next to Zara.

"Dad?" She said shocked to see him come in. She walks up hugging him.

Dennis grabs his daughter's head, bringing her in for a hug. His heart felt good knowing his daughter was okay. "You good?" He asked checking her out. "Everybody out." He instructed, seeing Phil's crew leave. Leaving Phil, Cameron, him, and Killa. "GO to the truck," he said seeing his daughter walk out with his bodyguards. In this moment it was either life or death. Dennis stood firm waiting forr Phil to make his mind up. "Do what you have to do," Dennis walks out the house, getting into his truck. He waited as he heard six shots.

The End......

About the Publisher

I understand the journey of being an aspiring author can be both exciting and challenging. My love for reading and writing fills my days with joy and purpose. As a mother from Indiana, I find inspiration in exploring the depths of romance, horror, erotica, and fantasy. It's a path that many of us can relate to, filled with creativity and passion.

Read more at https://linktr.ee/Cardihearts.

www.ingramcontent.com/pod-product-compliance
Lightning Source LLC
Chambersburg PA
CBHW021121130726
47988CB00003B/1103